SHE MAKES IT WORK

A DIY Guide to Thrive in Your Hustle

KATIE CORCORAN

KATIE CORCORAN

ISBN-13: 978-1502816177
ISBN-10: 1502816172

Photography by: Jonica Moore Photography

Cover Designed by Katie Corcoran

Printed by CreateSpace

www.katiecorc.com

FIRST EDITION

DEDICATION

To all of the hustlin' leaders, dreamer and action-takers out there who have paved the paths before this current generation. We are all thankful for your perseverance, dedication and showing us it is possible to follow our passionate dreams.

TABLE OF CONTENTS

KATIE CORCORAN

AUTHOR'S PREFACE

"Hi, my name is Katie and I have been addicted to being busy my whole life."

I am a self-proclaimed Lady Hustler. My calendar is full, my projects are overflowing, I like to take weekend trips —or longer ones when time permits—and I have a thirst for learning. I rock the grind because I love it. I love the masterful combination of productivity, drive and achievement. These three make up my personal self-fulfillment lovechild.

I suppose the need to be busy could be classified as an addiction, but it's one with positive rewards and helps fuel a desire to strive for self-actualization and progression {and what does being "busy" mean anyway?}. So if betterment is my high of choice, then I'm OK with riding the wave hopped up on the strongest dose of goodies {which typically come in the form of a great latte and some vitamins, but you catch my drift}.

I frequently run into "provokers" who challenge me to explain why in the heck I take on so many projects, work 14-hour days multiple days in a row, and add way "too many sides" to my main career dish. For the most part, I look at my aggressors point-blank in the eye, shrug my shoulders and say, "Meh, I don't know, I'm crazy." Then giggle light-heartedly and try to run away as quickly as possible to dart and dodge from further interrogation. The truth is, I never had an answer. The shoulder shrug was it.

I started to believe I truly was just different than others and I did the best I could to suppress my desire to try, try, and try again by creating two very different profiles of myself.

One part of me was the girl who worked her buns off in a corporate job developing digital marketing strategies for small businesses on up to Fortune 500 companies, while simultaneously partying like a champ because "that's how the advertising industry socializes, people!" I giggled and occasionally goofed off with coworkers, and basically tried to coast along with the rest of the "cool kids" to avoid having to admit to them, and myself, that I was meant to do something different. To break the mold. But when asked what I was doing on the weekend I'd typically lie and say, "Not much, just hanging," again to hide the truth about my side hustles.

Then there was the authentic and vastly different, me. I spent nights and weekends in my early to mid-20s fulfilling passions that, when looking back on it, somewhat amaze me to this day. I produced a music video for an artist {and fellow Lady Hustler in this book, Clara Lofaro}, became a lifestyle coach through the Institute for Integrative Nutrition, developed one-on-one coaching and group lifestyle programs for clients for my personal business, joined—and am growing—a direct sales business through a healthy living company called

USANA, wrote this book, developed a bi-weekly blog and still made time for friends, family, and travel throughout the process.

This happened in only three years.

Repeat: *"Hi, my name is Katie and I have been addicted to being busy my whole life."*

I remember going on a family vacation when I was in middle school, and we rented a pint-sized "van" to drive the six of us from town to town along the countryside in Europe. Like typical middle-schoolers, my three siblings spent the driving hours fighting over time to play the latest handheld video game and bragging over who made it to the highest level.

I, however, sat silently smushed in the back passenger seat in the third row, pleasantly peering out the window, pen in hand and notebook in lap, staring into space every few minutes.

"Kate, you're quiet back there," my dad said, with the intention of probably making sure I hadn't fallen asleep or was in a fight with any of my game-playing siblings. "What are you doing? Are you OK?"

"Yes, of course. I'm just analyzing and measuring how I will accomplish my goals for the upcoming school year," I said timidly as I realized how atypical that may have sounded coming from the mouth of a 14-year-old on a family vacation.

I create goals and fall in love with the satisfaction of

crushing them while simultaneously creating a lustful relationship with the next best move.

At an earlier age, during a New Year's weekend in sixth grade, I sketched an entire women's fashion line with platform shoes, tube tops and sparkly jackets {is that '90s or what?} I colored each strap, wrote descriptions for each piece and priced out the line in its entirety. I knew nothing about high fashion living up in the sticks in New Hampshire but, if you ask me, my line was quite trendy and affordable for any young teen to score and I was proud of it.

So proud that my scholar brain congratulated myself, while my shy, close-minded side hid the papers under my bed and never shared them with a soul. I was insecure, and felt my creative talent wasn't "good enough" to ever amount to anything, so this fashion line was a secret I kept to myself.

As an adult, I realize that I was the only person holding myself back from fulfilling my dreams. I was scared of rejection and questioned my talent and judgment. I was afraid to commit to the "outside the norm" projects I dreamed about.

It is too easy to get stuck in fear and self-doubt.

My drive, creativity and skills were there. The confidence, was not. I was afraid to break the mold and risk a comfortable status of "blending in." I was embarrassed to own my interests. I was uncomfortable being me. Even though I was always energized by my ideas and goals, I still buried my creative urges by remaining small and safe.

I spent college in Boulder, Colorado where the confidence meters ticked just a smidge higher than than before. I found myself blending into Boulder/Denver's fashion scene by working at a local boutique, interning at a Denver fashion consulting company and writing a regular column for a national college online fashion publication CollegeFashionista {founder Amy Levin is a fellow Lady Hustler in this book}. The fashion "niche" made me feel more at home, like I belonged.

After college, I rode that niche all the way to New York City and began "following my dreams" by working at a high -end jewelry label. In {many} moments of misery, it was there that I officially had my AHA moment. I was 22 and not happy. I wasn't living my dream. I checked my soul at the door every day before stepping foot in the building. It was in an over-controlling, under-appreciated work environment with no room to excel unless you viciously {and soullessly} played the political system.

I had moved New York City for more than that. After my AHA moment, the light bulbs started really firing in my mind. I promised myself I would never commit to activities, jobs, people, etc. that don't contribute to positive growth.

It's certainly true that NYC can chew up your bank accounts, rob you of proper shut-eye, and the intense culture can be intimidating. But I see all of this for its amazing opportunity and I get giddy thinking about the newness that unintentionally smacks you in the face—

sometimes multiple times a day. You always have to be on your toes and every day can feel like a vacation when you are open to all of the possibilities NYC has to offer.

It's not uncommon to see Lena Dunham shooting a scene for *GIRLS* (one of my favorite shows) on the way to work, or read online about a new exhibit or premiere you realize is open just a few blocks away, or perhaps see Jay-Z's car parked outside of the office after having seen him the night before in an opening concert at the Barclays Center in Brooklyn—all serendipitous moments I am humbled and awed to be able to drink up all of this excitement. It also reminds me that the world is our oyster and we can make our lives whatever we want it to be.

Opportunity exists every where we go, on every street corner, at 3 a.m. in a local bar, in line at a coffee shop, or even in the park when you take your pup for a walk. There are always people to meet and connect with. Nowadays wonderful opportunities can occur for anyone, no matter where you live. The internet and all the social medias have created the possibility of connected with people with similar interests all over the world. This connection can inspire you to reach your dreams, no matter where you live.

For someone like me, who loves the hustle, I thought I had to run off to the big city to put myself in a position to see activity and capitalize by joining in. But what I discovered after nestling into this culture is that the hustle is just a part of my being.

I find myself restless when idle. I thirst for inspiration from a new personal development book, exploration from new surroundings and I find pleasure in listening to a new podcast or trying a new workout. Are you picking up what I'm putting down? This word offers a multitude of opportunities for all of us. We don't have to be afraid to hone in on our interests and dabble in a few others.

So, "busyness" might be an addiction, but I know it's one shared by many ladies. I now meet like-minded ladies all the time. They rock the same addiction. They include student juggling multiple projects, entrepreneurs who've started their own product or service companies, musicians, branding consultants, owners of trendy on and offline publications, leaders of female networking communities, ladies rocking a side hustle alongside a full-time job, and generally inspiring people.

I call these women the "Lady Hustlers." They are everywhere…

I set out on a mission to discover what makes the Lady Hustler tick? How is she able to achieve all she does? What motivates her and keeps her motivated, despite challenges, self-doubt and fear along the way?

To answer these important questions, I interviewed numerous, successful Lady Hustlers and learned how each Lady "does it"—from productivity tips, essential routines, common habits and behavioral patterns. I combined these success tips along with common work/life balance trends I acquired by coaching stressed clients, and also paired by own "hustling" habits to empower you to ensure you are nothing short of happy in your own life.

My hope is after you learn about the Lady Hustler's day-to-day you will gain a better understanding of how you, too, can become that hustle-savvy, confident powerhouse you are meant to be.

This book will provide you with:

- Productivity hacks from 20+ Lady Hustlers

- Goal-setting exercises and how to manifest for your future desires

- How in the heck to still get shut eye with your crazy "to do" list

- Wellness guidelines to follow to ensure maximum energy level {i.e. more focus time!}

- The importance of maintaining relationships with positive mentors & cheerleaders

- How to be a boundaries-setting {and following} master

- The unique THRIVE every day concept

- Resources to get you rocking and rolling with your Thriving needs

With this book, you can become a work/life balance

master and gain a clear understanding of your own personal and professional needs. This will move you closer to becoming that badass, thriving Lady Hustler you are meant to be!

Here's how "She Makes It Work".

CHAPTER ONE: SHE'S A PLANOHOLIC

In order to keep her weeks in check, the Lady Hustler is the ultimate planner. She has both a digital calendar and a written calendar. She books her weekends with activities as far out as she can foresee. She can even tell you which day the first of the month falls on for the next three months.

The Lady Hustler know she has the power to shape her own destiny. Each new day presents her with opportunities to become a better version of herself. And she does this by planning the heck out of her calendar. A scattered schedule will cause her productivity levels to drop and allow for more distractions to take over. This is her time to make certain she is ready to rock each Monday morning as she remains in hot pursuit of her goals.

SHE HAS GOALS, AND LOTS OF 'EM

The Lady Hustler finds freedom and satisfaction in reaching her goals and continually stays focused on building her "ass-sets." She does this by pri-or-i-tizing her short and long term goals according to their importance. She plans on a weekly and monthly basis, with her annual goals always at the forefront of her mind. She schedules her calendar accordingly and "works smart" to reach her weekly goal by the end of the day on Friday. The Lady Hustler has figured out how to work "smarter not harder."

And how in the heck does she do this?

The Lady Hustler uses her innate skills and good sense to manage her expectations so she doesn't set herself up for failure and/or have to change her plan midstream. It's true that a large goal or passion can can feel overwhelming. By planning realistic "benchmark goals" and meeting each one, the Lady Hustler has the power to achieve the big, "I really want to do this, but I don't know how to get there" goal to find her passion in her hustle.

Let's say the Lady Hustler has a goal to find a new job and/or career. She knows it is probably too ambitious to reach this goal in one month. So, even through she may feel desperate to make this new change, she takes a "chill pill" and plans her incremental goals so that each day she is hustling and getting back to her new gig.

When the Lady Hustler accepts incremental progress she makes each day, she is primed to reach her ultimate goal. She avoids procrastination this way (the ultimate state of paralysis) by achieving her "mini-goals" along the way. Eventually, she is able to leave her job, ask for that promotion, start her own business, move, etc. This preparation is her "blueprint," that is her ace in the hole to achieve her dreams.

The first, and most important step for the Lady Hustler is visualizing where she wants her life to be in one calendar year. Where does she want to live? What does she want her work life to look like? Does she have a health goal in mind? Does she want to go back to school for another degree/?

Once the Lady Hustler is clear about her one year goal, she begins the task of realistically monitoring and analyzing her current lifestyle habits to to determine when, where and how she will be able to meet her goals. She then sets a deadline, followed by breaking that dance on down into reasonable increments that will work within the parameters of her lifestyle. For example, if she knows she has more time on evenings and weekends , she'll schedule French lessons for 45 minutes three nights during these times so she can practice her "bonjours" while still going to work or school.

The Lady Hustler has aspirations and she's not going to let time slip by her—sometimes chipped—fingertips. But, she's realistic about timing and knows how to plan the heck out of her work time. Then, she is more at peace with the outcome.

So why is the Lady Hustler so meticulous about planning out her goals?

She wants to feel like she has direction. She wants to feel grateful for her own achievements. She wants to feel pride in her work. Distinct, tangible forward progression doesn't come easily to anyone, especially because distractions can, and will, interfere with the Lady Hustler keeping her eye on the prize. The Lady Hustler must constantly check herself by checking in on her mini-goals to ensure she'll meet the big ones!

Ready to begin this exciting process?

DIY Tips

➤—→ Start with the big stuff. Start with your life goals. Picture yourself as a retiree. How do you want to feel about your past life? Where do you see yourself and what's your lifestyle like? (No regrets here, ladies.)

➤—→ Take some time to think about this and write ALL of your ideas down. Don't be afraid. Sometimes this feels so real to us that we often don't want to admit to ourselves we actually have desires. This is fear. Fear of not achieving, fear of admitting we are in control of our destiny, fear of taking our lives back into our own hands, an overall fear of failure. Do not succumb to fear! Be honest with yourself. That fresh notebook is itching to be filled with your wildest dreams!

➤ Next, organize your dreams into a five-year plan 10-year plan, etc. by thinking about the BIG GOALS you want to achieve. This may include having children; moving to your dream destination; switching career paths; developing and maintaining a marriage... These are your main goals from which you will create your shortened incremental yearly and monthly goals.

➤ Write your goals as SMART goals. SMART stands for Specific, Measurable, Attainable, Realistic and Timely. There are wonderful sources online that break down this acronym. {Learn more in the Resources section.}

➤ The one-year plan is the easy part. Another option is to take your goals and make a visual out of them by creating a dream or inspiration board full of uplifting quotes, welcoming colors and feelings and experiences you want explore this year. Then, you can post it where you will see it every day. It will remind you that each day holds the promise that you are closer to your dream.

LADY HUSTLER REAL TALK

"Maintaining my hustle means committing myself to taking one step every day to get closer to my dream of owning a successful business. I want to make a true difference in the world and give myself the financial freedom to create a life I love. Some days I have the energy and time to take leaps. Other days I can only muster up the energy to take baby steps, but what's important is that I'm constantly moving forward and growing into the woman (and entrepreneur) I was born to be."

MICHELA ARAMINI // Personal Brand Consultant & It Girl Mentor

"I want to use the Big Rocks example here. I figure out what is most important to accomplish today and pick one thing I have to do by that deadline. Then, I also choose something I really want to do—like go to a spin class, meet friends for dinner, etc. I do those things, no matter what. And then plan the rest of my day around the fun and the work. If I ever feel like "I don't have enough time to complete my tasks," then it's typically time to re-evaluate how effective I am with time management and/or if I am setting realistic goals."

KARA LEVINE // Pilates Instructor & Holistic Health Coach

"I always feel behind. I never feel caught up and always feel like I cannot possibly do all of the things I want to do. My 'to-do' list is overwhelming. I have a hard time balancing these things and prioritizing because I truly want everything in this life! I want to have it all, and I'm not quite sure that's possible, so this is an area I am working on—to figure out what I really want vs. what I think I want. This is something I have to work on and something that has definitely plagued me for a long time."

HALEY HUGHES BRYAN // Entrepreneur, Terrimae

"The two big things that have brought me more clarity in maintaining a thriving life are (1) not trying to do everything in a day, but concentrating on the most important long-term and time-sensitive things, and (2) balancing my day between business, music making/practicing/writing, and making sure I get outside and experience the day. I know I need to allow for break time to be the truly present in my work life."

CLARA LOFARO // Recording Artist & Songwriter

SHE SETS THE MOOD AND TAKES 30 ON SUNDAYS

Thirty minutes. That's all it takes to piece together the nuances, the ins and outs, the working jam seshes, the workout classes and the freedom to have fun time because, guess what?! The Lady Hustler has fun, too. (And lots of it!)

To make this happen she takes the time after a freeing weekend to light a candle, put on some thought-provoking tunes, take out that digital calendar and planner and schedule her "hustle" for the week. The Lady Hustler believes that "if it's not written down, then it's not real and probably won't happen." She starts by making a few goals for the week and scheduling time in her calendar to plan time to meet each mini goal.

Each goal will have "benchmarks" which must be completed to reach the ultimate goal. So, for example, a goal for the week will not be "finish, design and launch a blog" 'cause, "goodness gracious" that is a lofty and unrealistic goal to be met in just one week's time.

Instead, the first thing she does is take the larger goal and break it down into a list of smaller tasks. She schedules a time (say 45 minutes) to devote to each task and books them around her workouts, meetings, calls, etc., so the task will 100% be completed during the designated time. She then avoids those moments spent thinking "I should have done that" for "Thank goodness I've completed Step One in the process. Now on to Step

Two!"

The Lady Hustler devotes 100% of her attention to the task at hand to ensure she's making the best use of her time. Think of it this way: completing a task when it is scheduled could be the difference between finishing for the day at 5 p.m. instead of 7:30 p.m. The Lady Hustler knows the value of having "me time" at night, so you better believe she adheres to the plan and powers down work when the clock strikes five.

Next, after writing out a plan, she enters it into a digital calendar, scheduling appropriate time blocks to complete each benchmark. This way, reminder alerts will pop up to ensure she is held accountable when "out and about" and "on-the-go." Then, tasks will fly by with the ease of a checkmark here, and a checkmark there and, before she knows it, that computer will be powered down to move on to the fun stuff!

Lastly, it's important to note the Lady Hustler allows time let go and take some freaking pressure off. It may sound silly, but she values the importance of allowing for an extra-long walk in the middle of the day to, quite literally, stop and smell the roses.

DIY Tips

➤——→ Get to love your digital calendar! The constant reminders can appear overwhelming, but it'll become in handy when you realize you're only busy during the workday and you can visually reward yourself with free time. Schedule the fun stuff too! Most calendar apps have a digital interface that's quite beautiful on the eye, so you actually enjoy scrolling around and adding/editing items to your calendar and inviting others in on your adventures

➤ The paperback calendar is just as important as it aids in the "I'm going to crush my goals this week" mantra. Maybook.com is a fabulous resource to custom-build your own planner to keep by your side every day. You can do this with colors, fonts, styles (and even monograms!)

➤ Be realistic with your goals and begin to take note of how long these goals are actually taking you to complete. Are you setting aggressive deadlines that are clearly unattainable? Perhaps, allocating more time would allow you feel accomplished instead of overwhelmed?

➤ Save 30 minutes on Sunday for planning time. You'll be happy you did, and you'll be surprised at how efficient your feisty self can be when adhering to this master five-day, goal-crushing plan.

LADY HUSTLER REAL TALK

"My productive days start on Sunday. I need a few hours to get ramped up for the week ahead. I clear out my emails and listen to all of my new and saved voicemails. I make my lists and goals for the week. Then, Monday morning it's off to the races. Really, my productivity comes from outside of work. Eating breakfast is a must. Working out is a must (at least four days a week for me). And sleeping a solid eight hours is a must."

TALLY MACK // Lawyer & eCommerce Enthusiast

"My days are often busy, but in an organized chaos kind of way. I keep my work life detailed in my Google Calendar and also write out a short list of tasks I need to complete each day. I always check my emails first thing in the morning to make sure my team is set to go in both NYC and Chicago and they are getting all the support they need from me. The rest of the day depends entirely on what city I am located in, what time of year it is and all the other variables of an entrepreneur. While it can be a bit hectic at times, I am mindful if I freak out my team will freak out. So I stay as collected and organized as possible."

AMY LEVIN // Founder & Creative Director, CollegeFashionista.com

SHE'S MASTERED THE TIME HACK AND WORKS IN HER KFZ {KEY FOCUS ZONES}

Her work days are booked to a T. Not the kind of booked that's overwhelming, but rather the kind that makes the best use of her time. She works smart. She realizes what time of the day she is best able to focus on the important tasks and she plans those big projects around her key focusing hours. For example, if she has a larger project with a more pressing deadline, she knows that catching herself in that KFZ is imperative to giving the project(s) the TLC it deserves.

The KFZ is basically another way to play the "work smarter not harder" principle. But the bigger task is defining the proper KFZ at the individual level—essentially becoming aware of when and why her focus switch is sometimes powered on to the max, while at other times, she can't seem to remain engaged. In basic form this strategy will help her complete tasks in an organized manner when her lights are on, signals are firing, and creativity and drive are at their peak.

This KFZ varies for each Lady Hustler and focus time may even change according to the day of the week. Some ladies are typically very focused on Monday mornings, but may not be as focused on, say, Fridays. Perhaps this Hustler has attended some evening gatherings during the week, leaving her feeling completely spent by Friday. That said, she will not abandon her goals on Friday, however. Yes, she still has "it" in her, but she knows that

Friday may not be the best day to address her more challenging goals or benchmarks. The end of the week may be a better time for her to complete her admin tasks. This way, she can check some items off the list before she enjoys screaming FRIYAY and welcoming in the weekend!

The Lady Hustler knows her most productive times of day and days of the week and, to put it bluntly, she capitalizes on that shit. This reinforces the importance of her non-negotiable planning schedule. She sets up her week strategically to avoid foggy periods. She is NOT a fan of that unfocused, mushy brain.

For a bit of a reality check, there will be times when the Lady Hustler doesn't feel inspired to write that blog post or fulfill her designated time to answer emails. As a rule of thumb, she makes a commitment to complete the task within 24 hours so she doesn't lose her mojo. Flexibility is key to helping her keep sane while thriving in her hustle.

This requires discipline, but she makes it work {and you can do it too!!!}

To stay disciplined, the Lady Hustler is the ultimate resistor of the infamous internet browsing trap. She schedules her internet browsing during her daily "free time," only. Her free time is just as valuable as her hardcore focus time. Free time can include something as dull as paying a bill to stalking her Instagram favs. But she plans for it. She loves her time with beautifully positioned Insta imagery, searching for new music or emailing a friend from her personal account, because she knows spending time on her internet surfboard is the ultimate reward.

Take the "Power Hour" theory and flip it on its head with a 45-minute *jam* sesh and 15-minute "reward me" time. Some hustlers will get stuck in a working daze, which is also important, but she can admit her best work is complete during these strategically planned timeframes for the day.

Think of it this way... *If you lessen the time you have to complete a task and only devote your time to that task, then you better bet your bottom dollar you will buckle down and finish the task during that time.*

Working for 45 minutes and creating freedom around that extra 15 in her "power hour" tricks her into feeling like she's not on a complete leash and she can conquer the world!

She also knows that in an effort to really get the job done she is not staring down her inbox and spending the majority of her day communicating with others. Emails don't complete projects. They may help when delegating elements of the project to others, but they can be just another form of procrastination.

The Lady Hustler knows she cannot expect to move the needle on her goals if she's refreshing her Gmail all day waiting for an answer from a client or partner. She's in control of her time. She knows doing all of her follow-ups in the morning is the most time efficient to ensure she's freeing up her time to work on a goal. Then it's on to her KFZ time.

DIY Tips

> ⟫⟶ Identify your KFZ and schedule your large projects during that time. These are typically the projects that require deep thought.

> ⟫⟶ What's your poison of choice for "clutter time"? Social media? Shopping? Staring at your inbox? Learn how to identify this time and allow yourself some freedom to browse, but do so in a defined time frame.

> ⟫⟶ Emailing can become a time suck! When you have the energy, send out those emails. And if it's not timely, there are plugins and apps to allow for scheduling emails in your Gmail inbox. (Tool suggestions can be found in the Resources section).

> ⟫⟶ Another email hack is to set up a pause on your Gmail inbox. That way it will not automatically refresh itself the second an email comes in, but rather when you manually refresh. Then you can check your email in accordance with your schedule.

> ⟫⟶ Disabling email notifications on your phone is imperative to take control of your time. No one likes that person who's walking down the street reading an email that is not important at that time, weaving through dangerous traffic, to accept a calendar invite from her boss. Not cool, dangerous and definitely prevents you from

having the ability to enjoy the moment. Yuck.

→ If you're a music fan, log into your Spotify and configure a playlist or two that lasts 45 minutes in length. Then you'll know when your jam sesh is complete and you can give yourself a break for 15 minutes. Plus, you will hear some killer new beats

→ If music is a distraction, set the timer on your phone to 45 minutes and get crankin'. Also, try the Koingo Alarm Clock app and schedule automatic random reminders in your phone with messaging like, "Am I doing what is most important for me right now? Keep on track kiddo!" for an added motivation.

→ Let' face it. You know yourself and you know your limits. When you are fried, you know taking a break from the hustle is the best thing at that moment. Don't forget to honor your rest!

LADY HUSTLER REAL TALK

"The thing I find to be most helpful is an app called 30/30. You assign a task to each chunk of 30 minutes, and the app keeps you on track, letting you know when it's time to move on to the next thing. I'm not great at managing my time, and so this app keeps me accountable. Balance, for me, looks like setting aside time to work and time to play. I try to be extra productive during the day so I can fully relax during my time off. I need a really distinct work and play balance, and so I try to do a lot of one, and then a lot of the other."

STEPHANIE MAY WILSON // Writer

"When starting your own business, work takes up pretty much all of your free time. I assume this must be what it's like to have a child—you worry about him/her when you're away, agonize about every decision you make, and are constantly discussing its future with your [business] partner. However, like any 'parent,' sometimes you just need a break! So I've made it a priority to take my weekends back, which has been a lifesaver. I'll work more during the week, just to be able to go for a long jog or peruse the fruit aisle without panic on a Sunday.

And because I seem to have been bitten by this entrepreneurial bug, I've also started a wedding DJ business with my husband. Might sound like more work, but it actually gives us an exciting chance to spend time together and share our passion for music ... maybe next year I'll take up 'sleeping in.'"

JESS PETERSON // Founder & Creative Director, Mighty Oak

"Figure out when in the day you are most 'on' and tapped into your creativity, and schedule your side hustle time then. Because I'm more 'on' and creative in the evenings, I work on my business Monday-Thursday evenings and Sunday afternoons. I schedule my 'me time' for weekday mornings, Friday nights, and all-day Saturday. It's so important to take time for yourself to clear your mind and properly unwind. Some of my best breakthroughs came to me after an invigorating yoga class or leisurely Saturday in the park."

MICHELA ARAMINI // Personal Brand Consultant & It Girl Mentor

"I think taking periodic breaks in between accomplishments is really important. Even five minutes makes a huge difference. I am also big on list making. I often write things in my phone calendar to work on the next day when going to sleep. Then I'm ready to go in the morning. I try to keep it as realistic as possible."

CLARA LOFARO // Recording Artist & Songwriter

"My tip for a productive day is to not try to multitask too much, but focus on one thing at a time and do it fast, efficient and well. Then, quickly move on to the next and start crossing off the to-do list."

SARAH DEVRIES KURTENBACH // Consultant, Social Media & Startups

SHE KNOWS THE POWER TO CHOOSE IS IN HER OWN HANDS

The Lady Hustler is a creator. She molds, adjusts and morphs her plans to create a lifestyle to fulfill her wildest dreams. She also knows, however, that sometimes "life" can get in the way of her careful plans. She knows there is so much more to life she can't control but maintains a firm belief that the universe will somehow provide for her.

For example, the Lady Hustler had no control over the family she was born into and where she grew up. Her caregivers determined where she went to school and taught her values in their words and actions. For better or for worse (or somewhere in between) she adjusted to the environment that was provided for her.

The Lady Hustler is committed to lifelong learning. She knows that there will be bumps and bruises along the way. She views these challenges as opportunities for growth so that she can turn those lemons in to lemonade.

To create the "life she loves," the Lady Hustler knows that opportunity may arise in the strangest and wildest of situations! She is always open to possibilities even when one is not readily apparent. Example: Let's say the Lady Hustler is looking for a new job. She stumbles across a company that piques her interest and her first instinct is to check out their website and LinkedIn to see if they are hiring. If they are not hiring for a position that fits her profile and interests, she doesn't stop there. She uses her network to identify someone in that organization that she can talk to about the company and the industry. This web of connections is really the driving force behind her developing new opportunities.

She may feel shy or uncomfortable about doing this, but when she is prepared with genuine questions to scope out the company "vibe, she will find that it is actually almost "fun" to reach out! She talks to someone new, asks questions and learns from that new person {Repeat: The Lady Hustler knows that every interaction can be an opportunity for learning.}

To help with her sometimes awkward feelings, the Lady Hustler practices the "Law of Detachment" which, according to the Chopra Center,   teaches her the freedom to "be as she is and participate in everything with detached involvement." This law also teaches that "uncertainty is your path to freedom."

So what does that mean to the Lady Hustler? This goes back to her knowing that she has the power to choose. She knows that she cannot control someone else's response to her. She only has control over how she responds to the actions of another. She knows that when she "puts herself out there," not everyone will respond to her with positivity. The Lady Hustler has practiced the fine art of letting go of outcomes.

Example: Boss is taking abnormally long to answer your time-off request. Response: You know you have done everything in your control to demonstrate that you are a committed and hard-working asset to the company and team and you have earned your time off.

Example: New guy you're I'm dating doesn't seem to want to keep in touch as much as you do. Response: You were comfortable enough to bring the "authentic you" to the relationship and you can accept {after a time} that you were "not a good fit."

The Lady Hustler knows that obtaining the feedback she desires is not required for her to thrive.

Now, this may sound like a bit of a hopeless situation, and one could sit back and think, "Why should I reach out to others, or really ask for what I want? What if I continue to face rejection when seeking my true desires?"

Rejection is a necessary evil. But with the proper attitude and strategy, it's easier to get up and move on to the next best thing. This is no sugarcoating, but rather a reminder to feel empowered to go for the freaking gold! When rejected, the Lady Hustler does like Aaliyah and chooses to "dust herself off and try again."

When the Lady Hustler is in search of fulfillment, she closes shop every day with some added rejection chinks in her armor, but she knows that, while there will be challenges and rejections along the way, there will also be more opportunity for wins as well. She's all about that "winning" life.

DIY Tips

➤ Spend some time thinking about how you chose to respond to situations that were out of your control. (Think about your commute, work life, personal relationships, sweat time, etc.)

➤ How do you interact with the people in your current relationships? Do you become hostile if someone doesn't text/call/email/facebook message you within a few hours? Do you make assumptions about the other person's role in your interaction? Do you choose to just say "screw them" to convince yourself that you can positively detach from that person?

➤ Speaking of detachment, what does the Law of Detachment mean to you? How will you be able to detach from the outcome of situations that are out of your control? What will you fill that space in your head with?

➤ Write down ten daily choices you will make to detach from uncomfortable situation so you can improve your overall happiness and well-being.

LADY HUSTLER REAL TALK

"With great power comes great responsibility. Being an entrepreneur sounds glamorous and liberating, but it has to be something you do for the love of it and not because you think it gives you freedom or instant wealth. In many ways, it limits your freedom more than a regular 9-5. Knowing that my success/failure relies solely on my own decisions is a heavy burden to bear. Knowing that some days I am at the mercy of other people's whims and wants limits my own mobility is something I have to deal with constantly. So at the end of the day, knowing that I'm doing what I do for the love of it and not the money is what keeps me motivated and focused."

LIZZY OKORO // Publisher & Editor-in-Chief *BUNCH* Magazine

"My largest stressor is letting people down and letting myself down. There are moments I will get so overwhelmed that I feel like I'm having a panic attack and then I tell myself, 'Emily, just breathe. You are not saving lives and this is supposed to be fun,' and it all comes back into perspective. At the same time I tend to thrive from the stress. My tunnel vision turns on and I'm able to hone in on what needs to be accomplished and will get it done."

EMILY MERRELL // Events Manager, INTERMIX & City Society NYC Women's Networking

"I just have to remind myself sometimes that I can choose how much to take on, or how little to take on. It is OK to do nothing sometimes. Living in such a fast-paced and competitive environment like NYC makes it easy to forget that sometimes. Mostly all the stress I experience is self-induced. I am in every situation because I've chosen to be there. Also, you can't really control what other people do, but you can control your reactions. Stress is a reaction to situations that make you uncomfortable, and feeling stressed about it is a choice. I cannot say I always make the right choice, and I am definitely more stressed than I need to be, but this is something I'm working on."

JESSY DOVER // Creative Director & Entrepreneur, Dagne Dover Handbags

"I maintain the side hustle mainly for me. It's an amazing creative outlet that I own, and that truly makes me happy. However, since my side hustle includes 600 members in the community, I do of course feel pressure to make each event worth it, and continue to provide our members with value so they continue coming to events and spreading the word. I think if it stopped making me happy and a place where I could test and learn, then I wouldn't be able to continue with it, since the passion would be gone, and therefore, the benefit for my members."

MELANIE COHN // Social Media Manager & Founder of Young Women in Digital

"I am happy because I am in complete control of my life. I am not one to settle for what's easy, comfortable or expected. I enjoy challenges, which is why I chose to get into my own business. I am happy to get out of bed each day because I am loving the experience of MY JOURNEY. It is not anyone else's and that makes me happy and motivated each day."

HALEY HUGHES BRYAN // Entrepreneur, Terrimae

SHE'S REALISTIC WITH HER FINANCIAL GROWTH

This is simple. Rome wasn't built in a day. For the Lady Hustler to build her empire—no matter how glamorous or simple it will be for her—she knows she must be realistic with her finances. She must admit to herself that, as a multi-passionate passion-seeker, she still needs to find a way to make ends meet to pay her bills, eat healthy and delicious meals, get in some sweat time and have fun. To do this, she must be financially astute.

Sure, she's been known to splurge here and there on a trip or rack up some credit card debt after finding that stunning pair of must-have shoes, but she's aware of the types of financial "splurges" and "savings" she needs to keep her in a low(ish)-stress financial situation.

As nice as it would be to have a constant flow of that dough, the Lady Hustler engages in constant reflection to determine exactly what "wealth" or "success" means to her. Is it being rich in experiences—ranging from something as simple as a weekly morning walk with a group of local girlfriends or spending a bit more paper on a trip? Does "success" mean having a big bank account? For some, the latter is the ultimate goal. It's important to understand that there are many people make money nowadays, some of them quite unconventional. The Lady Hustler needs to know where she fits and where she places value on this important question.

For most people, it's more comfortable to receive money

for their time and talent. Most jobs are structured this way, which provides less risk to the employee and employer. The employee shows up to work, completes the work and gets paid by the employer. A win-win for both parties. Troubles arise, however, when one party does not hold up their end of the bargain. The company may over-promise a salary increase, promotion, or the opportunity to take on additional roles, but fails to deliver on these promises. Or, the employee accepts a job for its compensation package, only, and neglects to look at the big picture of what it means to work in that particular industry or office climate. Perhaps the corporate culture conflicts with the employee's morals; or she has to make too many sacrifices (ie: a longer commute), which makes her feel dissatisfied with her job.

Other ladies choose a non-traditional route, where they just say, "screw it, society" and take on a variety of roles to fulfill their basic living needs and accrue savings. It can seem glamorous to take on the "fly by the seat of your pants," approach but the downside is that the cash flow is less predictable, with highs and lows throughout the year. There is little stability and no paid time off, health insurance, tax deductions, retirement savings (like 401k) or business expense write-offs. The self-employed worker makes many financial sacrifices in exchange for the freedom to design her schedule and time.

The passion-seeker could also opt for the third work option and rock the "side hustle." Many Lady Hustlers work a full-time gig which helps them pay the bills. This is a fabulous option when trying to test the waters to determine if a side passion will pay at the lifestyle level the Lady Hustler desires.

The Lady Hustler and her peers have a variety of interests and fall into a number of job categories. The difference is the Hustler is in tune with what she needs from work to feel fulfilled. That conventional 9-to-5'er lady is going to feel just as empowered working as a member of a team than another non-traditional "let's roll with it"-type if they both feel valued as a team member and are progressing in their goals to reach ultimate fulfillment?

On her quest to achieve fulfillment, the Lady Hustler faces doubts {just like the rest of us}, but she does a pulse check to see where these doubts are coming from.

Are they money-related and will this influence her happiness?

Does she thinks she is incapable of taking on new responsibilities?

Does she feel worthy of the work assigned to her?

She realizes she may face a cutback in her expenses or be faced with adjusting her lifestyle. If this is the case, she knows that transition won't come easy and she commits to treating herself with "mini gifts" along the way, perhaps in the form of a $15 weekly manicure or a meal from her favorite restaurant. She then learns how to practice feeling like she has "enough" with the life she's developed. This allows her to accept all "gifts" with gratitude. The Lady Hustler works hard {and so do you} and all humans deserve moments to treat themselves to something that makes them smile.

The last, money concept the Lady Hustler wholeheartedly adheres to is the balance between cutting back on expenses and finding ways to make more cashola {who doesn't love a good hustle?} She does her best to remain non-emotional in the short term and puts detailed thought into how she can grow more stable financial and emotional wealth to support herself in the long term {or sustain her lifestyle}.

Where there's a will there's a way and the Lady Hustler finds her way to make her financial situation work whether she is creating her own wealth or relying on a dream corporate opportunity. She counts her blessings and knows that each day presents new opportunities. The Lady Hustler is grounded in her ability to recognize that she has everything she needs to attain her goals.

Financial wealth will come her way when she trusts that her "everything" and her "world" are right in front of her. She is satisfied with her own version of thriving.

DIY Tips

➤ Think about what wealth and success mean to you. How are the two interrelated? How do they remain in balance for you?

➤ When will you feel content with your wealth?

➤ When will you feel content with your success? In other words, what drives you and what are you striving for to feel successful?

➤ Think about times you've made less money but felt happier ... how were you able to stretch a dollar in that time of your life versus how you view a dollar now?

➤ Curious about additional mind-sifting reads about wealth happiness? Definitely look into Robert Kiyosaki's *Rich Dad, Poor Dad* and Kate Northrup's *Money, a Love Story*. Both are excellent reads that dive deeper into money-making strategies and may help you better analyze your relationship with money.

LADY HUSTLER REAL TALK

"I am constantly struggling with not living up to my own expectations. I definitely face challenges when trying to 'sell my coaching services. Overall, I'm really best at just being Malene, both professionally and personally."

MALENE ARVIN // Health Freak & Activewear Fashionista

"My biggest stressor is perfection, which is absolutely self-inflicted. As a new entrepreneur the biggest and most valuable learning curve is embracing the process and letting go of perfection, which only poisons the present. Growing a business alongside a full-time job means you have to embrace organic growth and be OK with the fact that a dream business takes a positive mindset and patience."

MICHELA ARAMINI // Personal Brand Consultant & It Girl Mentor

"The expectation to be great and the best artist & songwriter for me is immense. I have to constantly remind myself I am exactly where I need to be today. Sometimes that journey requires doing gigs and jobs I don't particularly find exciting, but my passion is in music and this is where I plan to stay. "

CLARA LOFARO // Recording Artist & Songwriter

"My largest stressor right now is to be able to support myself and my lifestyle financially. I recently quit my day job and relocated to a much less expensive area, and I know that I will create the wealth that I desire—just nervous that it may take a bit longer than I would like."

ANDREA HOOD // Health Coach & Business Mentor

"Money is always on my mind. It's hard when you're unsure of where the money is coming from in the beginning or if it will come at all. But to be honest, when you show up and do the work, all falls into place. It's just challenging to recognize this truth."

GURAMRIT KHALSA // Holistic Health & Soul Nourishment Counselor

"Money and finances are a huge stressor for me and sometimes it keeps me from focusing on the bigger picture. Learning the skills to really own my value and realize I'm worth every penny is so important for my mindset and growth. I need to create a plan. I am a fly-by-the-seat-of-my-own-pants kind of gal, so learning how to create a better plan is a challenge I'm tasking of myself this year."

BRANDI SHIGLEY // Turning Dreamers Into Doers & Founder of Fashion Denver

CHAPTER TWO: SHE'S GOT THAT R-E-S-P-E-C-T FOR HERSELF

Lady Hustler masters her time by maximizing her productivity during the day. She's got that going for her and while that's all fine and dandy, she has one thing that's generally the most important fact of all: She preaches like Aretha and R-E-S-P-E-C-T-s herself. She completes tasks not just because she wants to, but because she seeks the emotional satisfaction of feeling accomplished. She gets a high from productivity and knows exactly what routines, workouts, food and people must be included in her day to make sure she is incorporating the TLC her mind and body need to thrive. She is aware and knows how to be the ultimate listener to numero uno: herself.

This concept can be often be misinterpreted as selfishness, but the Lady Hustler knows that in order to live a balanced life, she has to flip the Golden Rule right on over and treat herself with the same gratitude she'd use to support a best friend or a fellow Lady Hustler. For example, she'd be as encouraging as possible when she sees her friend put her heart and soul into preparing for a speech. She'd let her friend do a mock presentation in front of her; provide constructive criticism and offer the utmost support before her friend embarks on the presentation date. She would even call her beforehand and/or send a good luck gift.

Society teaches us to have respect for others, but the Lady Hustler also knows how to have respect for herself ... 'cause damn, girl, that stuff takes balls! She has confidence and she clears her mind and spirit by incorporating a number of lifestyle "tricks from the chicks" into her everyday life.

These tricks include, getting good, healthy eats with good peeps, incorporating lots of movement and also mastering her gut-listening skills. These acts of self -R-E-S-P-E-C-T take this lady from a life coaster to a hustlin' son of a B.

Every busy lady is out there trying to get her hustle on, running from a meeting to an event and then back again the next day. There's often little time to stop, reconnect and center herself to remember the respect that's required within her to keep moving forward. It inhibits her from being present and available in the moment. This is how the Lady Hustler thrives. She takes time between the hustle to stop and smell the roses.

SHE IS HAPPY TO SEE HERSELF IN THE MORNING

The Lady Hustler wakes up on the right side of the bed most mornings and realizes each day is a blank canvas. She's planned the necessary "to-dos" in her calendars so she doesn't have to spend wasted energy on the happenings in life she can't control. There are 101 things she can't control so she focuses on the things she can control. She prepares herself every morning with a calm sense of routine before entering an unpredictable workday.

Her morning routine is her best friend—even if it used to be the bane of her existence in a past life {Hello, college}. She doesn't rush her tush to the office, class, or other commitment setting anymore. She digs the feeling of getting up slowly, incorporating a workout, stretch time, journaling, meditation or some quality time with her significant other. This puts her mind in the best place to be productive and focused. Even though her hustle is tremendously important to her, she knows she is only capable of producing her best, quality work when she is relaxed, her mind is clear and she can hop right into the grind without distraction.

She respects the time she needs to reboot and recharge and, for the most part, she doesn't wake up with a sense of anxiety and stress. She doesn't check her email accounts the second she wakes up {unless faced with an extreme situation, in which she certainly gets a pass}. She doesn't jump right out of the sheets and hop in the shower at the last freaking minute to get her booty out of the door. She take her sweet, well-deserved, time.

As an added layer of respect, she is conscious of her personal style and takes pride in looking presentable. This presentation is not rooted in the desire to impress others. On the contrary, she's learned that when she feels and looks her best, her brain has the power to be at its sharpest as well. If she has meetings planned for the day, she'll dress the part to an even higher degree so she can radiate that confident strut when talking her talk to meeting attendees and/or clients.

Some days she pulls out all the stops. Her favorite statement necklace, a few bouncy curls in her hair to add volume, and rocks those "comfortable" heels. Again, it depends on the tasks she needs to complete during the day, but she makes sure she feels and looks the part for whatever task is ahead.

To add to her routine, she may do something as simple as allowing stretch time in the morning or planning one coffee date each week with a friend to lighten the mood before heading into the office. With extra time, the Lady Hustler begins her commute with a gigantic—and often contagious—smile on her face. She has devoted the time to relax in the morning to boost her confidence levels and get the "I respect myself" signals firing in her brain.

DIY Tips

➤ Think about your morning routine: Do you snooze through multiple alarms then rush through your shower routine, run out the door, (breakfast in hand), only to find you've missed the next train or notice you don't have enough gas to make it to your required destination on time? These extra, unplanned minutes have made you late. {"Crap!").

➤ If any of these scenarios seem like you, then you have gotten yourself in a bit of a routine trap and it's time for some reevaluating. The adjustment in your morning may take an additional 20 minutes, but that could be exactly what you need to manage your stress.

➤ Think about a simple adjustment you could alter in the morning to provide you with additional time. Or, if your mornings are already on point, then perhaps think about switching up your commute to work, encourage yourself to try a new coffee shop or perhaps tune into a new podcast. These easy and manageable adjustments will help you feel like you're getting down with your bad self and starting anew each day.

LADY HUSTLER REAL TALK

"I usually have some sort of coffee meeting in the morning that is a mixture between business contacts, inspirational friends, or mentorship discussions. I love starting out my mornings sitting over coffee and bouncing ideas off of people."

SARAH DEVRIES KURTENBACH // Consultant, Social Media & Startups

"I have a firm morning routine and make sure yoga is included in my routine every single day. Even if it's just 20 minutes. Spending time to focus on the spiritual aspect of hustling really grounds me and keeps me on track since I've set an intention to calmly reach my goals. Sometimes we all need to just slow down, feel our feet and engage our cores to feel like we have our heads on straight."

GURAMRIT KHALSA // Holistic Health & Soul Nourishment Counselor

"My hustle means taking care of me. I won't be able to help others if I am not helping me. I am often called on for my opinion and expertise. I really take the time for myself and work very hard at creating balance. I want to be the best example of myself. I want to walk the walk—

talking the talk is just words. Actions are what I am about."

KATHY BACON // Radio Host & Voice Professional

"Typically I wake up and start my day with a 10 to 30-minute meditation. I follow that with journal writing to try to clear out the fog and begin my day with awareness. After that, I usually check emails and get my music business stuff out of the way before heading to the studio."

CLARA LOFARO // Recording Artist & Songwriter

"I wake up really early—before the sun most days—so I can have my alone time. I meditate, do some personal development reading while drinking warm lemon water, walk the dogs, get in a workout myself. I find that when I start my days like this I am super productive."

ANDREA HOOD // Health Coach & Business Mentor

SHE NOURISHES HER BODY TO FEEL GREAT

Here's the good stuff. The Lady Hustler is generally a healthy eater and realizes the way her brain functions is indicative of the quality—and quantity—of munchies she puts in her body. She knows a meal consumed solely for instant gratification will get the best of her in 40 minutes' time. A healthy salad filled with rich and raw whole foods will keep her tum and mind full through the afternoon. On the contrary, a bagel will dub as a "filler" as its speedy glycemic release will leave her feeling unfocused and will chemically create an afternoon crash and a craving for coffee or sugary treats to keep her "satisfied" till dinner. No thank you!

Believe it or not, in addition to all the planning that occurs on Sunday, the only way the Lady Hustler knows she won't fall victim to the "doughnut for breakfast" game is by building a meal strategy for the week that's pleasing to her taste buds, easy on her wallet, and convenient for her to lug off to work.

Again with the Sunday planning {Goodness gracious!}. But this is so important for the lady powerhouse because she is self-sufficient and knows bringing the goods to work will allow for greatness to ensue when she's on her grind. Also, this helps her have some control over the decisions she makes during the day. It's much easier for her to default to her homemade delish salad and not give in to temptation by opting out of the fatty takeout burrito entree her counterparts are chowing down. She's already prepared the darn thing, so quality, clean ingredients it is! As an added bonus, she saves a buck—or $13—on an expensive lunch when enjoying Mama Hustler's home cookin'.

The Lady Hustler also knows that a major paradigm shift occurs when readily available natural and organic foods are just a hop, skip and a jump away. There shouldn't be any question about the quality of food she incorporates into her diet. In fact, farmers markets are on the rise so making meals and having snacks on hand should make supporting the local community a cinch. Some will object and label these "local/organic" items as expensive or inconvenient, but the Lady Hustler knows price ain't a thang when she's got health on the brain. In fact, doing research about local and organic foods will help her locate these healthy snack hot spots and also find stores or markets where they are most affordable.

One main trick she incorporates into her food shopping regime is purchasing non-perishable and longer-lasting items like whole grains, nut butters, oils, and beans/legumes during a "bigger shop" one to two times per month {Note: All good foods will spoil, including those listed above, but nuts, grains and oils don't spoil as quickly and won't have to be consumed at the same rate as produce.} This way, the staples remain on hand for longer periods of time and can be cooked once at the beginning of the week and leveraged as meal prep for the rest of the week. If perishable goods, like seasonal produce, are on sale and looking mighty fresh, they can be purchased in bulk as well.

For example, say the Lady Hustler is in the mood for a peach-infused smoothie in the wintertime. Well, good thing she stocked up on organic peaches from the farmers market in the fall, cut them up into bite-sized pieces and set those babies in the freezer for a winter slumber. Her motto is, if they're on sale, keep them on hand and save them for a later date.

She knows herself and knows her worth {Thanks Drake}, so she seldom allows herself to consume a cheaply made, lifeless meal. Her groceries at home are vibrant and she uses high-quality ingredients to prepare her meals for consumption for the week. Her calendar may not have her specific meals written down, (because even the Lady Hustler knows that may be taking things a bit overboard), but she knows that if she washes, chops, dresses and/or cooks before the clock strikes Monday she is going to have one healthy week!

If she can get a good three days of breakfast and lunch planned on Sunday, then she considers this a well-rounded batch of food for days one to three. She will prepare Thursday and Friday's lunches later in the week to ensure the ingredients are fresh to def. Plus, then she can create new meals to avoid repeat dishes.

So what exactly are good, whole foods? Essentially anything that has one ingredient. Yup, that means no bagged, boxed or packaged BS. She instead prepares beautiful creations out of multiple whole foods. A rule of thumb is if the ingredients are difficult to read, the product probably has added fillers and icky stuff that our bodies don't know how to digest.

In addition, she nourishes her body with a high quality supplement to ensure she's reaching optimal nutrition levels while consuming the healthiest foods available.

Then there's sugar. The Lady Hustler is aware that sugar is disguised as hidden ingredients in many processed foods, which makes it especially difficult to avoid. {Think sauces, milks, salty snacks, most breakfast foods, or anything that ends in "ose"}. She realizes, however, that to tame her sugar cravings she must incorporate healthy fats, protein and at least one serving of fruits and vegetables into each meal. Fats and proteins will help keep blood sugar levels stable to avoid that extreme, obsessive feeling of "needing sugar … like, now."

The Lady Hustler is aware when she's making emotional food decisions when feeling overwhelmed or stressed. When she's getting that urge for an afternoon bag of chips or finds herself rummaging through the office kitchen cabinets, she knows how to do the "stop, pause and rollout."

She often realizes the craving is caused by a deeper issue and the food she craves will never fill the void within. Perhaps her boss made a comment she didn't like or she's in a strange place with a friend or loved one. Maybe she's crashing after being caffeinated all morning following a night of major partying and little sleep.

She uses this moment to identify the void. She loves a good challenge, so getting to the bottom of this conundrum is actually quite pleasing. Much like completing a goal, she enjoys the emotional satisfaction from figuring out why she has these cravings.

This is when she asks herself, "Am I causing further harm by shoving a double-chocochunk cookie {or three} into my mouth? Is this item the most nutritionally dense food for my mind right now?

For the most part, the Lady Hustler opts for her own version of a "treat" and enjoys a classic Granny Smith apple.

DIY Tips

- What does your current food plan look like for the week? Are you allowing yourself to succumb to the daily cravings that may not be healthy for you? How do you feel during the workday when you're eating a bunch of yuck versus taking charge and eating the good stuff?

- Here's a Holy Grail of a mantra: Eat well today, feel mutha lovin' stellar all week. Boom.

- A few food prep hacks to consider:

    o Buy the non-perishable foods in bulk.

    o Wash and chop veggies in advance to easily cook up or throw over a bed of greens.

o Make multiple meals at the beginning of the week while you already have all the ingredients spewed out on the counter and repurpose with new species and in new concoctions each day.

o Cook grains once each week. Most grains take about 40 minutes to cook, so it's recommended to cook them while chopping your veggies to optimize your time.

➤ Fun fact: It takes about three hours to digest a meal, so keep that in mind when stuffing more food into that fist-sized stomach of yours. Pow!

➤ If you're new to learning about organic vs. non-organic produce, it's worth becoming aware of the Dirty Dozen and the Clean Fifteen to better understand which fruits and vegetables are safer in non-organic form and those to only buy from the organic section (more information in the Resources section).

➤ When shopping for vitamins, look for the most potent. They should have been clinically tested for absorbability, pureness and safety, and should be sourced from raw ingredients. USANA HEALTH SCIENCES is the best and most transparent company in the industry. {Learn more info in the resource section}

➤ Having trouble guzzling down enough water?

Pimp it with some fruit or cucumber for added flavor and sip out of a beautiful BPA-free bottle.

➤ Think about the sugars you consume per day. Do you notice you have a sudden crash an hour or so after you eat an item containing a high sugar content?

➤ Suggested fix: Keep it real. If it comes in a box, make sure you find whole ingredients, including 100% whole wheat, sprouted wraps, and whole grains and seeds. Your body will thank you later.

➤ As a rule of thumb, do like Michael Pollan and: "Eat food. Not too much. Mostly Plants" and you'll be golden.

LADY HUSTLER REAL TALK

"If the body and mind are in a balanced, healthy state, you can face the biggest obstacles, handle a crazy-busy day and still be your own best friend."

MALENE ARVIN // Health Freak & Activewear Fashionista

"I have definitely learned to listen to my body and I know when I physically and emotionally need to slow things down and disconnect, even if it's just for a day. Your body knows when you are heading towards burnout and will give you physical signs, such as fatigue or illness, or emotional signs, like negative thoughts. Your body and mind shut down and you're unable to move forward in your business. So intentionally tuning in to your body every day is incredibly important."

MICHELA ARAMINI // Personal Brand Consultant & It Girl Mentor

"Right out of college I would feel guilty if I wasn't always working. I thought if I took time for myself or to be with friends and family that I was falling behind on the growth of CollegeFashionista. I now realize I am more successful when I have a balanced life. Working out, getting dinner with friends and spending uninterrupted time with my

parents is so important to me. When I neglect those things I am not as productive in my business.

AMY LEVIN // Founder & Creative Director, CollegeFashionista.com

"I strive to take really good care of myself. I eat well, take my vitamins, exercise five-plus times a week, and have a passion for health and fitness. However, I know that just because you eat right, it doesn't make up for averaging five or so hours of sleep a night. It's something I really struggle with, and know that I need to make that more of a priority in my life."

SARAH DEVRIES KURTENBACH // Consultant, Social Media & Startups

SHE MAKES THAT BOOTY WORK

This is an important one and much like that non-negotiable morning routine, the Lady Hustler works it out, y'all. She doesn't view exercise in a "must do five miles five times per week" kind of way, but rather incorporates 45 minutes of a fun activity on a regular basis to get her heart pumping and help her get a kick ass session in her KFZ. She needs to physically sweat, and boost her serotonin to deal with stress. This, quite literally, helps her to "not sweat the small stuff" when she's hustling in her grind.

She keeps things interesting by diversifying her workouts to make sure she's changing things up and trying out a variety of activities to move her tush. Yoga classes, spin classes, a brisk outside walk, runs, bike rides, jump roping, and stretching keep her on her toes before and after the workday. An important thing to note is the Lady Hustler is not hard on herself about working out. Instead, she moves because she knows that the power of movement is imperative to influence her well-being and it helps her achieve that much-needed release.

And guess what? Much like her meetings, the Lady Hustler puts her workouts into her calendar. Sure, she may be tired on Friday, but she's planned ahead with at least three workouts early in the week to give her the freedom to be flexible later in the week.

Remember that 45/15-minute principle utilized during the

workday? The extra 15 can be filled with a walk around the block, stretches in the office, or perhaps a short breathing exercise. Remaining sedentary is harmful to the muscles and joints and is, ahem, killing us softly. As age begins to take over, the body requires a longer cycle to wake up, so continuing to move those legs is tremendously important.

In addition, instead of having yet another coffee or "drinks" meeting, catching up with a friend over an exercise sesh is a fantastic way to discuss the latest and greatest in one another's lives while sneaking in some movement at the same time. In fact, humans are more inclined to push themselves harder when working out with other people, which holds true for workout classes as well. The energy, drive and motivational nature of group exercise classes provides the support the Lady Hustler desires during her sweat time.

Movement comes in many forms and it's easy to forget that keeping active during the day doesn't have to be about the crazy luxury spin class or an intense run. Instead, taking the short stints of time off to disconnect from the technological world will help you re-engage with the real you.

Collect your thoughts, get lost taking in the scenery around you and train your brain to open itself up to thoughts outside of the stressors at work. In the moment, daily obstacles may seem like the greatest drama, but in the grand scheme of things, taking care of numero uno is most important. Then you can brush that dirt off your shoulder {in most situations} and move forward.

DIY Tips

➤ If you are not the type to do a heavy workout in the morning, getting up even 15 minutes earlier each day to incorporate a quick walk or stretching and yoga will provide a refresh of the mind before rushing into the day. There are free apps and guided yoga sites, so testing out the digital workout world may be a good fit for you (suggestions in the Resources page).

➤ Sign up for classes ahead of time. Affordable and/or free new member trials are a fantastic way to try out a new workout style. Plus, since you often have to "sign up" in advance, you have to be held accountable to make it to your sweat sesh on time.

➤ Get social with it! Haven't seen a friend in a minute? Instead of meeting for a typical Happy Hour date, encourage a friend to attend a class with you or catch up while conquering a brisk walk. The change in setting may spark a new, inspiring conversation.

➤ Create a bumpin' playlist that will make a workout more enjoyable when you're movin'.

➤ Incorporate at least 150 minutes of exercise, at varying levels and frequencies, into each week.

This gives your body the ability to recharge, but also taps into varying muscle groups within the body's kinetic chain.

LADY HUSTLER REAL TALK

"Most of my stressors in my business and life are caused by myself so I make sure to delegate well, go to the gym to blow off steam, and consistently eat well for my body."

TALLY MACK // Lawyer & eCommerce Enthusiast

"I have a 'no-excuses' list. I know working out every day in some form keeps me sane. Sometimes I am more lax about it than others, but I know without it every day, I will not be happy or as productive as necessary. Sometimes this requires planning ahead, like packing a workout bag and finding a class time that fits around my schedule, but it's all worth it to have a healthy, well-rounded life."

TAYLOR ROCKOFF // MA of International Development & Yogi

"My mentor always tells me you can do some things well, but not everything. My craft is smart design, and creative concept development. I fuel my creativity by doing some form of exercise everyday! Sometimes it's SoulCycle, sometimes it's yoga, sometimes it's a long run. Whatever the form, it allows me to be in peak mental condition, which is necessary when running my business."

JESSY DOVER // Creative Director & Entrepreneur, Dagne Dover Handbags

WHEN HER BELONGINGS ARE IN A CLUTTER, HER MIND'S A CLUTTER

Much like the importance of giving her body the respect it deserves, the Lady Hustler values and appreciates her belongings and her living space. This includes organization and giving her "stuff" the love and respect it deserves.

Her home is kept tidy. She strives to leave it in a state that's clean enough to entertain in the event she has any unexpected guests. This leaves little room for embarrassment with its current state of presentation. She's comfortable with a dish or two in the sink, but won't let a whole tower of ickiness pile up over time. She puts all of her clothes away at the end of each day or before leaving for work in the morning and makes her bed so her domain is fresh when she arrives home.

As for interior decorating, she does the best she can to make rooms in her home feel clutter-free and beautiful. A desk loaded with bills, unread magazines and junk creates stress on the mind each time she looks in that direction. These are the projects she has no interest in tackling after a productive workday. She reads letters and pays her bills on time to avoid backup and stress caused from having finances hang over her head.

Though she may not necessarily be a guru when it comes to Feng Shui, she is drawn to decorating her rooms to reflect the emotions she wants to feel when spending time in each space.

Perhaps she wants her bedroom to feel tranquil, natural and calming to take her back to memories where she's felt most relaxed in nature. Or, she may want her office to have words of inspiration, higher ceilings for growth and expansion, louder colors and/or more natural light to keep her alert and focused.

The Lady Hustler knows that by incorporating an errand here and a little tidying there, she'll make these mundane tasks seem more manageable over time as well as declutter both her out-of-home needs and within her humble abode.

DIY Tips

» ⟶ Make your bed every day and keep your room clean. This is a simple act and you'll be happy each day when you arrive home and your space is organized.

» ⟶ Clean your dishes while cooking so the task doesn't appear too daunting after you've enjoyed your (healthy) meal.

» ⟶ There are great Feng Shui introduction books to teach you alignment, color choice, removal of clutter and how simple alterations can create energetic emotion in a space.

» ⟶ Respect your personal space. Perhaps test

something as simple as placing fresh-cut flowers on the dining room table. It will add a new color scheme, and could provide some unexpected cheer.

LADY HUSTLER REAL TALK

"I shower EVERY morning, and get fully ready for the day. I think Oprah said when you look your best you feel your best (don't quote me on that one, I'm not sure) ... but the general idea really stuck with me. Even if I'm tired, or overwhelmed, I make sure to take the time to make myself at least look presentable (even if I don't quite feel it). Fake it 'till you make it!"

JANE CORBETT // Graduate Student, Clinical Psychology

"I'll have a few weeks that are exhausting. Maybe it's a convention. Maybe it's a huge project or a deadline. Whatever event triggers it, there are some days when I get to work that I just can't function. I have no creativity left. Those are the days that I go through the motions. I complete what needs to get done and then throw in the towel. Head home early. Organize my apartment or do necessary chores before the weekend. Take a nap. Watch a movie. Do my nails. Me time."

TALLY MACK // Lawyer & eCommerce Enthusiast

YES, SHE STILL GETS SHUT-EYE

This one's a toughie. When others are admiring the nuances of how the Lady Hustler really "does it," they often question if she's getting the shut-eye she needs to function during the day.

"No, like really? Do you actually sleep?"

The truth is, some nights she has to stay up later than planned. For the most part, she knows the minimum number of hours she needs for her to stay alert and alive during the day. To that point, it's important to be aware the happy range for most is between six to eight hours per night to experience long term health benefits.

She doesn't need her mom to tell her how important it is to get enough sleep. Instead, she takes control of this responsibility herself. Much like her necessary morning routine, she conducts a nightly wind-down which includes turning the lights down low, washing up and doing her best to refrain from screen time. It takes time for the human eye to adjust to natural darker lighting so it's important to have a slow adjustment period to embark on a lengthy slumber.

Technology and TV time is a habit. Habits can be broken in as little as two to three weeks. If sleep is lacking, then that tech life may be the cause. Take note of screen time. This may be contributing to 'night owl' syndrome.More restful sleep = a brighter and more energized day.

DIY Tips

➤─→ Nip that Instagram/Facebook/Twitter scrolling before bed in the bud, hon! Social media will be there tomorrow and surfing could take your mind to unnecessary places. Then, before you know it, you've been lost for 45 minutes when you could have been sound asleep. Instead, you're thinking about something unimportant.

➤─→ If you need some kind of "entertainment" in the evenings, turn off all of your lights, pop in some headphones and listen to an uplifting and calm podcast, TED Talk or audiobook.

➤─→ Meditate and/or practice breathing exercises. That old "counting sheep" theory really does work to gain control of the mind.

LADY HUSTLER REAL TALK

"I am a morning person and get up at seven without pressing "snooze." Most days I jump out of bed, head to my living room floor and do just five to 10 minutes of exercise and/or stretches. It's the best way to start the day. At the moment I'm in a plank-loving period, so the current morning program is 10 minutes of planks, while I catch up with the world through morning news."

MALENE ARVIN // Health Freak & Activewear Fashionista

"It's all about the work/life balance. Sleep is very important to me and if I need an extra hour, I'll take it. Call me a prima donna, but I can't be productive without a good night's sleep. That's non-negotiable."

TALLY MACK // Lawyer & eCommerce Enthusiast

"My largest stressor is stretching myself too thin and not getting enough rest. I have the tendency to drive myself to the point of exhaustion."

SARAH DEVRIES KURTENBACH // Consultant, Social Media & Startups

"I do my best to eat healthy and light food throughout the day. I refrain from drinking alcohol or eating a big meal at lunchtime because I know it will tire me out and I won't have the fuel to focus afterward. I try my best to allow myself to rest when I need to. There's no sense fighting fatigue. I work hard so I deserve time to rest and recuperate."

CLARA LOFARO // Recording Artist & Songwriter

"Always sleep. I don't believe in 'Team No Sleep.' Getting seven to eight hours of sleep helps ensure that you are healthy and ready to focus. There will be some days where sleep is not an option. If you're truly working efficiently, you will find that you can sleep."

LIZZY OKORO // Publisher & Editor-in-Chief *BUNCH* Magazine

SHE BELIEVES IN A GOOD "DISCONNECT"

Disconnecting from Technology addiction is one of the most difficult and overwhelming addictions to overcome. The Lady Hustler loves to share moments in life with loved ones across the world through phone conversations and social media. When connected, she also gains the ability to instantly respond to a text while listening to a podcast, refreshing her email and taking a quick snapshot of a beautiful sunset within a whopping 15-second timeframe.

But, alas, there are downsides to constantly checking email, staring at screens and picking up a device to fill "Real Life Moments" with Instagram scrolling or email refreshing. Ah, yes, the joys of real life.

The Lady Hustler doesn't like losing these moments. She values time spent with her friends at brunch and resists the urge to check "lord knows what" on her phone when her friend momentarily excuses herself from the table to use the restroom. She practices mindfulness. Takes in the moment, enjoying the sounds of the restaurant and monitoring the tiny details otherwise ignored when distracted by a screen.

There are two main reasons the Lady Hustler believes in disconnecting from technology.

1) Disconnecting allows for greater, quality human-to-human connection,

2) Disconnecting is for personal self-fulfillment when she is by herself.

The Lady Hustler could easily spend 14 hours per day looking at some type of screen. First it's the alarm on her phone in the morning, followed by email checking then Instagram looking. On her commute, she's streaming a podcast or music, then reaches the office where she's typing away and surfing on a screen the majority of the day. Then her night routine may include some type of phone conversation, catching up on personal email or streaming the latest Netflix series. And just like that, the screen time has hit a maximum for the day.

The Lady Hustler makes a choice to take in her surrounds beyond the screen. She values midday walks with music or even music-free {Gasp}. She knows she is more productive using technology for work when she is able to disconnect when she's not at work. Plain and simple.

At the end of the day, she strives to remain honest with technology use. She is aware of her personal vs. work technology time and values a good ol' fashioned disconnect.

DIY Tips

➤───→ Have a phone check before entering a social engagement and leave your phone in an inaccessible place until after the event—or politely bring your phone to the bathroom to check your internets while sprucing up.

→ Challenge yourself to take in your surroundings. Be mindful. Don't fear looking like you are "alone." Instead, cherish this alone time.

→ Take note of your routine and how technology plays a role in your daily activities. How can you adjust to perhaps eliminate even one hour? What would you fill this hour with? Think about the time and space you will be able to embrace with this extra seven hours per week. Love it!

→ Birds of a feather flock together, so set an example to rebel against the urge to use technology. If you reach for your phone, you are giving others permission to do the same. Remember two wrongs don't make a right. Lead by example and put away that device when you're with a loved one. Chances are, they'll follow your lead and refrain from refreshing their feeds in your presence as well.

LADY HUSTLER REAL TALK

"This summer I nearly hit my breaking point. I was in meetings all morning, there was some sort of fire drill {at my old job} and I had to catch a plane to Charleston. I jumped in the cab with my friends and I literally told them not to talk to me as I sent orders to our creative team and sorted out some trivial problem. I felt broken, exhausted and frustrated. Sometimes I look at my computer and think, 'Why the fuck is this important? How am I changing someone's life? {That's a whole other conversation}.' Anyway, I was bitchy to my friends. I was so consumed with work. I sat away from them on the plane and when I landed I looked outside at a world free from skyscrapers and the thickness of humidity in the air. It felt like someone released me from my cage. I felt freedom for the first time just by being away from it all. I realized there are other ways of living."

EMILY MERRELL // Events Manager, INTERMIX & City Society NYC Women's Networking

"Sometimes I put my phone on silence and completely disconnect from the world. I can get serious anxiety over constant contact via phone/internet with people/fans/colleagues, even friends and family. When this happens, I usually peace out."

CLARA LOFARO // Recording Artist & Songwriter

CHAPTER THREE: SHE'S CURIOUS AND STRIVES TO BETTER HERSELF

The Lady Hustler loves some good old fashioned playtime. She enjoys time spent with others and makes sure she puts herself out there to create memories outside of the confines of her "to-do" list. She puts that phone on silent and gets down with her bad self by going to dinner with friends, dancing at night, brunch on the weekends or testing her curiosity through random adventures on a Sunday. She deserves to disconnect, a chance to peel her eyes away from the computer screen to spend quality time with the ones she loves.

She takes her fun as seriously as she takes her work by letting her hair down, painting her nails blue and putting on flash tattoos. It's her free time, ya'll, and the Hustler is ready to milk it for all its pleasure.

The difference is, she continuously commits to fill this time with self-betterment. She seldom spends her time chilling on her couch and instead places value in filling it with experiences to learn and grow. This is part of her thriving recipe.

SHE MAKES TIME FOR IMPORTANT PEOPLE

Good people mean everything to the Lady Hustler. It's clear she's created a life that helps her function with poise within her own domain, but she knows she must make time for fun to keep her happiness meter high.

She's not opposed to rearranging plans to coordinate time for her besties and values the moments she spends with others. Harvesting strong relationships helps her rebuild and recharge her batteries through a good laugh sesh or a long, deep conversation. There's nothing like having someone understand her, flaws and all.

She identifies people whose personality traits and morals make her feel expansive and alive, and she makes sure to deepen the relationships with these people. Acquaintances will come and go in her life, but she holds on to the good ones. These are the people she could be out with at night, or spend time laughing with when caught in the rain together. The "go-with-the-flow-when-you're-together" types. The ones who would drop whatever they're doing and bend over backwards for her just as much as she would for them. Songs remind her of them and the memories they created together. They are the people she'd have just as much fun going on an extravagant trip to Thailand with as she would realizing she just ran out of gas in her car and laugh as they pick up the pieces.

Think of maintaining relationships as if they are a piece of yummy—and healthy—pie. No matter how you slice it, there's only so much to go around. So, for example, the more people included in a love pie, the smaller a slice {aka love and attention} you can give. But fewer close relationships bring larger and better-quality slices to share. It has the crust, filling and, for an added bonus, some additional whipped cream on top! It's the real stuff. The Lady Hustler may know many wonderful people, but she chooses to give the biggest slices to those who deserve to share with her the many flavors of life.

She prides herself on seeing the glass half full and she only hangs out with "on the bright siders." No one has any room for negative individuals.

Again, this stems back to understanding that the Lady Hustler has the ability to choose her own happiness. Which also means she chooses the people who will influence her life. She may appreciate and respect the thoughts and opinions of others, but only she knows what is best for her. She keeps her positive eye on the prize

DIY Tips

➤ Think of a situation where you felt most expansive alongside your best friends. What were you doing in that moment? Replay the scenario in your head. Were you in your home? On a vacation? Out at night?

➤ Then, recall how you felt with this best friend. Were you laughing uncontrollably after discovering you had to completely shift your plan for the day due to weather? Did you feel inspired to take on the world after sharing a vulnerable side or inquiring about advice? Put this feeling into words. Was it freeing? Comforting? Did it feel like a release?

➤ If you haven't connected with your "besties" for awhile, reach out to them and plan a catch up. Good friends make us feel happy. Besties share an indescribable bond and it's important to make sure you surround yourself with these lovely folks on the reg.

LADY HUSTLER REAL TALK

"I'm often way too busy, and sometimes I catch myself not having the time to slow down and just live. When that happens I feel sad. 'Cause it's so important to live and breathe. Then I will have a long chat with my man, call my mom or a best friend, and just talk about life for a moment."

MALENE ARVIN // Health Freak & Activewear Fashionista

"Spending time with my friends is so important for me to thrive. Talking to them about their days allows me to better understand the challenges we all face, and it also helps me realize that what might have seemed like a huge catastrophe earlier in the day, in the broad scheme of things, was really just a misstep. We can get so caught up in our own responsibilities that it becomes difficult to refocus. Count me in when planning activities with friends, whether it is dinner, wine on the couch or trips outside the city."

JANE CORBETT // Graduate Student, Clinical Psychology

SHE DOESN'T HAVE FOMO & LIVES YOLO TO THE FULLEST BY HAVING PASSIONS AND REMAINING CURIOUS

If the Lady Hustler could be described in one word, it would absolutely, positively be *passionate*. She gets up in the morning and believes each day is the first day of the rest of her life. She seldom experiences FOMO {Fear of Missing Out} because, to her, the grass isn't always greener on the other side. Instead, she's growing her own garden and establishing roots in activities that make her smile. She is in control of her own gatherings and won't waste her time feeling like others are living a more fulfilling existence. She doesn't look at social media accounts to compare their so-called "life" to her own, but rather utilizes browsing to influence her next fun move.

@AdventureGirl321 is at a mosaic tile-making class —"Sweet, sign me up."

@BeachBabe9821 is doing yoga with her mom in an early morning Saturday beach yoga class—"Yup, doing that!"

@HealthyFoodGal2728 is cooking a new kale-inspired guacamole—"Um, yum! Better have a gathering and invite my friends over to give this new dish a spin."

@ThisIsMyPar-Te25 is dancing the night away at the city's newest hottest spot—"Yup, doing that too!"

Though she may not be screaming YOLO {You Only Live

Once} from the rooftops, she truly lives by this credo and she'll be damned if she doesn't experience new things regularly. Those around her inspire her as well and she enlists her tribe of other thriving, curious friends to experience these new activities together. The memories created are ones she cherishes.

She has hobbies. They stem from being involved in her yoga community to plowing through novels on a rainy day. She knows what excites her and she keeps her mind open to finding new potential interests during her travels. She asks a crap-ton of questions. She's not doing this to fill space or to be annoying, but she genuinely wants to learn about the people she meets and the places she visits. She knows there's no such thing as a silly question and thus she is a sponge for learning.

With that, she takes the time to learn about her finances —even if they make her eyes cross—and enjoys learning various ways to diversify her income streams through investment strategies and perhaps a side grind. She learns about her taxes, legal nuances when having her own company to save her tush down the road, and about current events going on in the world. Again, these topics may not be as glamorous as the "Who Wore It Best" section in a magazine, but she strives to understand the important topics {to a point that she may even come to like 'em!}.

She tries new things and will be damned if she gets caught becoming sedentary or stuck in her ways. She'll take a new route home from work, stop at a new coffee place in the morning, try a new recipe at home, or talk to a stranger who's reading a book that looks interesting on the train. But in all seriousness, the Lady Hustler is multi-passionate and she continuously strives to remain curious. This is one of the main differences between her and those who stand by and watch her ride her own radical wave.

She is no different than a passerby. She is no more or less talented, smarter, wealthier or better equipped for success than anyone else.

So what's the difference?

She is curious. Curiosity is what helped her discover her passion. Her passion fuels her energy.

She had to kiss a lot of frogs before landing on her princes of passions.

The planning, the healthy eating, the exercise and the routines are all fine and dandy, but the most successful ladies are only able to thrive in their hustle when they have gratitude and are open to new possibilities. She recognizes life's pleasures beyond the "work" successes. She's successful because passion is what fuels her drive, but she is constantly on a quest to seek self-improvement and, as we now know, only harvests relationships that add to her growth and keep her shedding a positive light on the world.

DIY Tips

➤ What are the things that spark your interest in life? For example, what do you do during your browsing time online? Are you reading fashion blogs, searching for new recipes and inviting friends to your home to test them out? Are you planning parties? Searching for new music artists to share new tunes with your friends?

➤ What have you been putting off learning or enjoying because you haven't allowed for this hobby to grow? Write down five out-of-the-box interests you have and make a commitment to try one new hobby each month.

➤ When you make a new discovery for you, how does that feel?

➤ What do you do to make you happy during your free out-of-office time? Are you a movie buff, a sportsaholic, or do you spend lots of time outdoors? Have you ever thought about revolving your career around these passion points? If so, what are the steps you can take to make this happen

➤ What are your most valuable strengths? When people say "Wow, you are so good at that" or "You have such a natural talent for (fill in the blank)?" Perhaps take a look into those personal skills inside of you and utilize them to build a profession, side hustle or hobby around these traits

LADY HUSTLER REAL TALK

"I want to get out of bed each morning because I have a passion for learning and keeping my eyes open to newness. I love meeting new people and listening to their stories, educating young generations on what is truly important, and working hard physically and mentally toward new goals. There is a song that I listen to a lot in the mornings that was my 'wake up song' every day one summer at camp when I was younger. Travis Tritt's 'It's a Great Day to Be Alive" never fails to set the positive mood for the day."

TAYLOR ROCKOFF // MA of International Development & Yogi

"I am excited to explore anything and everything until I can find something that makes me happy. I still don't know what that means yet. However, I am mostly happy day to day, and in the bigger picture I can see that I am on my own path ... and for that I am proud. I am not afraid. Entrepreneurship is very hard. No one said it would be easy, but I have certainly taken the tough road by entering this world alone, against all advice saying otherwise."

HALEY HUGHES BRYAN // Entrepreneur, Terrimae

"I love running YWD because it actually has an impact on my peers' lives. I've been responsible for introducing people to new skills which have helped them get a promotion or a new job, and met a number of new friends along the way. It's extremely rewarding and fulfilling. I also love that YWD gives me a place to experiment with ideas I can't do at work. I'm my own boss and get to make all the decisions—that's liberating.

MELANIE COHN // Social Media Manager & Founder of Young Women in Digital

"Maintaining my hustle means never losing focus or drive. Some people see me as successful so it reminds me to be as hungry and determined as I was when my projects were just a far-off dream. The one piece of advice that I continue to reference is to never lose that spark. Never get too comfortable/lazy. Always push yourself further than you think you can go."

LIZZY OKORO // Publisher & Editor-in-Chief *BUNCH* Magazine

"I'm extremely ambitious and have about a million ideas, so it feels like I never seem to have enough time to do all the things I want to do. It can be frustrating when my ideas are greater than the amount of time I have to accomplish them, but I just keep moving forward every

day and know it's important to me to be a multi-passionate person."

STEPHANIE MAY WILSON // Writer

SHE HAS MENTORS AND A LIKE-MINDED TRIBE

This is a big one. Much as passion drives the Hustler to keep moving forward, there's no doubt in her mind she wouldn't be able to learn and grow if she didn't have an A-team of like-minded folks to bounce her ideas and "life lessons" off of. The Hustler does her best to be free of ego and can admit when she feels she is headed in the wrong direction. She captures pitfalls in a net and discusses a pivoting strategy with her mentors before they have the potential to turn into larger problems. Amen to that!

The Lady Hustler demonstrates strength, courage, poise and happiness, and she ensures her tribe exhibits the same qualities so both parties are able to lift one another, when needed. Mentors help pose scenarios that may differ from the Lady Hustler's day-to-day thinking so she can keep her mind open to take charge when a similar scenario arises for her in the future. A mentor can see a situation much more objectively. Achieving peace of mind is just as valuable as gaining a mentor's wise words.

The underlying message here and philosophy she follows —whether she knows that philosophy actually exists or not—is a belief in *ubuntu*. This South African philosophy translates to human connectedness and kindness toward others. It's a "we are people because of other people" approach. In the simplest form, this means the Lady Hustler has a group of cheerleaders and it doesn't matter where they are, all that matters is she finds connection with people who have qualities she admires. She wants to learn from people who have life lessons she respects. These mentors are her Oprah.

She keeps such a strong team of mentors that she enlists different mentors for various desires within her lifestyle. Perhaps one mentor has strong leadership and team management skills so she seeks traits and guidance when shaping the careers of others in her own organization. Or she may admire another mentor for her ability to dive deep into her personal relationships and aid with navigating dating or the up and down nature of an intimate relationship.

It's important for the Lady Hustler to keep in mind that while she has many bad-ass women who inspire her, she also has the ability to inspire others. She has her own unique views and invests just as much time listening and coaching others as she does being coached by her mentors. The Lady Hustler opens her mind to acquire guidance, with cheerleaders and mentors alike to ensure she's on a constant journey of learning and growth.

DIY Tips

> Think about someone you admire. What are the personality qualities about this person that make you gravitate toward them? Are they qualities you think you could gain through their guidance? Does her title or level of success interest you?

➤ Be introspective. What are the grey areas in your life where you feel you could benefit from mentoring? Find a person who is an "expert" in that area in your network. Reach out to them and offer to take them to coffee/tea. They will be flattered you reached out and it will be an eye-opening experience for you.

➤ On the contrary, is there anyone you feel you could take under your wing? You may end up finding you learn just as much from them during your discussions as you do from a mentor.

LADY HUSTLER REAL TALK

"I like to surround myself with two important groups: (1) A Board of Directors {ie: mentors} who are older, wiser and smarter than you in different areas who can help lead and guide you. Seek them out for their advice and strategy. (2) A Group of Celebrators—these are people who encourage you, build you up and lift you when you need it. They celebrate with you during your wins and encourage you during your losses."

SARAH DEVRIES KURTENBACH // Consultant, Social Media & Startups

"I remind myself why I do what I do for encouragement and for motivation, but having a support system is essential when I'm in a self-discovery phases. I have friends and family who support me in very different ways, and each are essential to keep me moving forward."

TAYLOR ROCKOFF // MA of International Development & Yogi

"I think something truly phenomenal happens when we band together as women, and that's what I'm creating with The Lipstick Gospel. My favorite part of my day is answering emails from my readers. I'm constantly amazed at how they invite me into their lives by sharing their own

personal stories. It's an honor to get to be a big sister to women I've never even met."

STEPHANIE MAY WILSON // Writer

"Choose to love. Be grateful. Be kind. Be compassionate. Have empathy and always remember the Golden Rule: 'Do unto others as you would have them do unto you.' And, of course, 'Be the change you want to see in the world.'"

KATHY BACON // Radio Host & Voice Professional

"CollegeFashionista has grown because our team has grown. I have found incredible hard-working and loyal team members who believe in the brand as much as I do. They bring skills that I don't have and challenge me on a daily basis to push CollegeFashionista further and further. I strive to be a strong communicator and couldn't thank my team enough for their drive and support."

AMY LEVIN // Founder & Creative Director,
CollegeFashionista.com

"Don't forget to smile and laugh and most complications are never the end of the world. Be kind and don't forgot your manners. Always be thoughtful. We are all busy, but time is precious and people are choosing to spend their

time with you, so make sure to be present and value them the way they value you."

EMILY MERRELL // Events Manager, INTERMIX & City Society NYC Women's Networking

SHE KNOWS HOW TO HAVE FUN ALONE

The Lady Hustler is not afraid to spend time alone. She values her free time free from outside distractions and sparkly objects. This enables her to reflect and recharge her batteries. Here she can {finally} take a deep breath and just plain chill the eff out for a second.

In these moments, she finds her innermost thoughts and feelings will emerge. Her creativity is given the space to open up and shine for all it's worth when some of the "thought muck" is sorted in her brain.

The Lady Hustler often finds her "greatest idea ever" is discovered when on a run, in the shower, or just before bed when she's able to dial down the voice running through her mind at other times of the day.

Spending quality alone time is not only valued, but it is also a non-negotiable constant in the Lady Hustler's schedule. She finds it fun and fulfilling to schedule activities for herself and by herself. This is when she can truly be "her."

DIY Tips

➤ When was the last time you spent time alone with yourself? True, raw alone time. How did you feel in this moment? What emotions surfaced for you?

➤ If it is hard for you to spend quiet time alone, you might want to start with five minute periods. There are so many distractions in our busy lives that it can be hard, at first, to completely quiet your mind. This will take practice, but the positive results from this daily commitment can be fantastic. Think about three good times in your day that you can remove distractions and focus on yourself. What will you do with these distraction-free zones? How will you have fun in these moments? Your mood will vary each day, but achieving aloneness is crucial to identifying the real, authentic you. {Welcome home!}

LADY HUSTLER REAL TALK

"If you really want something, you can make it happen. Even if you're busy, even if you have a ton of shit to do. Be OK with being imperfect. Be OK with letting some things slide. It's OK to be a bit selfish in order to be the best version of you there is. Because in the end, you being happier doesn't make you selfish. It makes everyone around you happier as well."

KARA LEVINE // Pilates Instructor & Holistic Health Coach

"I am also learning, albeit struggling, to be a great relaxer and TV watcher. I know this technically isn't a hobby, but on the weekends I consider it 'me time.' The most ideal night for me is being alone, watching Sex and the City and drinking wine. Did I mention I need to be alone? I'm a wildly social and curious person but there is nothing like having the apartment to yourself or lounging in bed for three hours reading and snoozing."

EMILY MERRELL // Events Manager, INTERMIX & City Society NYC Women's Networking

"I went to a yoga retreat recently and one of the lessons was, 'Where there is concentration, there is happiness.' This seems like a simple concept but rings true. When what you are doing has your full attention, when you can bring your mind back to the moment when it wanders

and do your best at what you're doing, it brings quality to your work, you are satisfied and not worrying about the next thing you need to do. It's simple. You are happy."

CLARA LOFARO // Recording Artist & Songwriter

"As an INFJ-A, I am considered an introvert, and as such, my alone time is very important to me! I usually dedicate one day a week to creative research and development, which means I spend the whole day alone with my thoughts. Believe it or not, my productivity is much higher those days than any other day of the week. If I can't get my alone time for one reason or another, I always have my noise canceling headphones with me as a good backup."

JESSY DOVER // Creative Director & Entrepreneur, Dagne Dover Handbags

THE WORD "FAILURE" IS NOT IN HER VOCABULARY

A challenge is like a drug for the Lady Hustler. She is addicted to the high of hearing "No," which then helps her uncover her fire that turns on a killer "Yes." The Lady Hustler is not without fear, however. She doubts herself just like anyone else. She just takes this doubt and turns it into positive energy for exploration and discovery.

Internally she may think:

Q: "Why do I feel this way?"

A: "I am nervous people won't like the message I want to share. Or what if I don't live up to my own standards?"

Q: "What is the root cause of my emotional feeling right now?"

A: "Is it fear? Yes, it is fear. I don't want them to think my idea is {insert unnecessary negative word here}."

This is where she stops to actually think about the meaning behind the question and taps back into her "why?"

"Why am I here?"

When she engages in negative self-talk she reminds herself of her ultimate goals and flushes that negativity down the golden throne. She faces her fear and identifies strategies to help her face this fear head on. She may listen to a motivational talk or consult with another Lady Hustler for encouragement.

So, what does she practice to get herself back into a positive place before reaching the point of no return?

She first takes inventory of the common culprits that spiral her mind into a negative place:

"Have I had restful sleep the past few nights?"

"Have I been exercising?"

"Have I been eating nutritionally dense foods?"

"Am I overwhelmed with my workload, personal emergencies, or friendship/relationship woes?"

When she has evaluated these basic human needs and her head is feeling more clear, she's ready to shift her mind out of the fear/failure zone by evaluating and following these top strategies to harness positive self-talk:

1.) Back to choosing. She chooses to understand some things are just plain out of her control

As much as she may want to adhere to a strict social calendar, diet, workload, etc., she knows there's a fine line between what she can and cannot control in life. But she knows she has the power to choose to be in a good mood. It's a hard practice to implement at all times and in all circumstances—but she chooses to face adversity when it comes her way.

2.) She respects her gut feeling... it's always right!

When it feels like her emotional "checks and balances" system gets in the way, the Lady Hustler can sometimes fall victim to allowing her head misguide her initial gut feeling. If going out to "just one more event" or offering to take on "just one more project" at work don't feel right, then she doesn't commit. She will be happier in the end and approach the "tough times" with her rational hat on.

3.) She knows she is exactly where she needs to be today

She lives most freely when she releases this unnecessary "perfectionist" pressure. The path can feel windy, but each twist and turn leads her to new discoveries. (More on this later)

When following these "positivity hacks," the Lady Hustler best harnesses her ability to remove the negative and hone in on what IS working for her.

Therefore, if headed into a direction that's "not working anymore," instead of looking at the scenario as a failed experience, she instead learns from it, pivots and moves forward with the new plan.

Then, with a clear purpose and removal of fears she is able to thrive. Nothing will stop her from attaining her own version of success!

DIY Tips

⟫⟶ Think of what fulfillment means for you. (This is your "why.") It may be uncomfortable to be honest with yourself, but stick to your gut and listen to your inner voice. Write this down in a journal, in your phone or email it to yourself.

⟫⟶ What challenges have you overcome and conquered on your own? {Wonderful!} Have gratitude for each of those successes. Write them down and take note of how overcoming each obstacle made you feel.

⟫⟶ What challenges have you avoided because you were afraid of the possible outcomes? Write down what specifically makes you fearful. Then visualize how you will feel when you overcome this fear in the future. You can do this. When you visualize a feeling, you will be better able to remain firm in your quest to achieve it.

LADY HUSTLER REAL TALK

"An easy mistake that many founders make is to not fully understand their brand position—and yes, I am guilty of that as well. When I started Mighty Oak, I was extremely passionate about creating customized branding experiences for starting female founders. While I loved the work and my clients, I soon realized that the time-consuming services I was offering were often out of my target audience's price range. Though frustrating at first, I realized that the problem wasn't with their budgets, it was with my incorrect position in the marketplace. I spent the end of 2014 reevaluating Mighty Oak's position and figuring out ways that I could elevate the brand, hone in on our services, and still support the women I so admired. I read a book called Make Your Mark: A Creative's Guide to Building a Brand with Impact, *which talked a lot about finding a solution to your client's challenges. And when Emily [my business partner] and I revamped the company into a stop-motion studio, the book gave me the idea to start our branded iPhone video workshops for female founders—empowering them with tools to create the content they wanted but couldn't otherwise afford. I think it's really important for other aspiring entrepreneurs to know that you CAN and SHOULD evaluate your position, all the time. It doesn't mean that you've failed, it just means that you're paying attention."*

JESS PETERSON // Founder & Creative Director, Mighty Oak

"It's not what happens to you, it's how you CHOOSE to respond to it. There was a time in middle school, where my dad was driving me to school and I was telling him how a girl in class had made me 'so mad' the other day. After my story, my dad just looked at me and asked, 'Sarah, did she really MAKE you mad? Or, did you CHOOSE to be mad?' Even at a young age, I understood that I had chosen my anger, instead of choosing to forgive. I've never forgotten that."

SARAH DEVRIES KURTENBACH // Consultant, Social Media & Startups

"Be generous. This is something I've been talking about with a lot of people. There are many people who hold their cards close to their chest as they're climbing a ladder or growing a business. They make a connection with someone and don't want to share, for fear of losing what they've just gained. But what I've found is that there's more than enough to go around. When we're generous with each other—with time, and connections, and ideas—it all comes back to us tenfold. Be generous. That's what I try to do."

STEPHANIE MAY WILSON // Writer

"My mom always told me: 'You don't get what you don't ask for.' I think many young women are afraid to even ask for help or speak up with their thoughts because they think they will come across as bothersome or annoying.

Well, if you don't ask for it, you can't complain about something not happening! That's my motto. I'm not afraid to ask people questions or for help and see what happens. What's the worst that could come of it? Someone says 'no'. That's really it."

MELANIE COHN // Social Media Manager & Founder of Young Women in Digital

"'Feel the fear and do it anyway.' I keep that written on a Post-it at my desk and use it to remind me how to make decisions every single day. It makes me feel like there's nothing I can't accomplish."

KARA LEVINE // Pilates Instructor & Holistic Health Coach

SHE TRUSTS HER JOURNEY AND PRACTICES MANIFESTING POSITIVITY FOR THE FUTURE

In the traditional sense, manifesting means "evidence of" or "proving" a scenario that has already occurred. The Lady Hustler plays a bit with the meaning of the word and dances on over to her future self to positively feel the feelings NOW of a potential reality down the road.

She does this by analyzing her goals and turns those present dreams into a future reality by visualizing the feeling of achieving the end goal in mind. Essentially, she puts herself in the shoes of her future self.

What will it feel like when running through the finish line of that first 10k race?

What would it feel like to assume a desired promotion?

What would it feel like to complete that certification or degree?

Then, when assuming this positive feeling, the Lady Hustler pulls all the stops necessary to use that energy to power through the "mini wins" and/or daily commitment required to manifest this future accomplishment.

This may sound a bit "out there," but the Lady Hustler knows it works. She has prospered when her hard work has met reality. She embraces the ups and downs and practices finding beauty in the low moment for growth.

She is an appreciation master and believes in each of her accomplishments. She believes in enjoying the fruits in her life. She is a dreamer and a doer and when she FEELS this confidence she is better able to keep her eye on the prize to achieve her goals.

DIY Tips

➤ Think of this as a "what if" scenario. What if you decided to eat a doughnut for breakfast every single day instead of a less sugary option? How would this make you feel? Would you be productive at work? Would you have the energy to make it to the gym at the end of the day or would you crash and want to head home, turn on some Netflix and head to bed?

➤ On the contrary, think of a job or class you took that you did not like. Did you meet someone you wouldn't have crossed paths with before if it weren't for the company {yay, new friends!}? Did you gain skills you were able to apply to future roles? Was it so draining for you? If so, are you better able to be appreciative the upside of your current job? Meditate on that for a moment. Sometimes the grass is just as green on this side as it is after traveling to the other side.

➤ One tactic to help with manifesting your positive future is to create a dream board and hang it in a prominent place. Pinterest and Instagram quotes are fine and dandy, but displaying your personal creation will provide you with a positive daily visualization of your hopes and dreams. This is manifesting for the future at its finest.

➤ In addition, write down your big goals too! It's OK if it's not achieved the first time you write it down. Life is not always about planned accomplishment. But if you write it down and the universe becomes aware, it's quite possible this opportunity may arise "unexpectedly"

LADY HUSTLER REAL TALK

"Writing is an art, but it's also a craft. The more you do it, the better you get. So to me, especially on days when words are particularly hard to come by, I remind myself that I'm doing some heavy lifting as a writer. I get better by the day, and that's a really great thing to be able to say about your day job. When it contributes to your dream, you know you're in the right place."

STEPHANIE MAY WILSON // Writer

"With Blush [health coaching], I love that I'm creating something new and, watching it grow. It's definitely a challenge because I've never started a business before, but it's almost like a game each day. What will I accomplish? What will I build? What will I discover? It's an ever-changing, challenging process that is allowing me to grow in so many ways. And of course seeing clients get real results makes me the happiest."

KARA LEVINE // Pilates Instructor & Holistic Health Coach

"My largest stressor is thinking about how to make my passions unify to create a logical life story. This is tricky when you have more than one interest in life, but I don't dissuade from having that. Most of my post-college life has not been the typical path one takes {ie: I didn't graduate and get a 'real job'}, and it has been hard to fight against social norms. It is challenging to continue to

push against those norms and stay 100% confident and optimistic that all will be successful in the end. I say it is all worth it. But it is not an easy road to take."

TAYLOR ROCKOFF // MA of International Development & Yogi

"I go, go, go because I want to be successful. I want to show the world that I'm strong and one day reach a point where I will let go of the doubt in myself and the negative self-talk. I sometimes believe that everything great will come but the best thing is right here, right now."

MALENE ARVIN // Health Freak & Activewear Fashionista

"What makes me jump out of bed? Knowing that every day is a new day. There are big decisions to make. The future of the company rests on the choices we make right now. We're still a startup, and we're almost above water. It's fun. Exciting. And most days, a little scary."

TALLY MACK // Lawyer & eCommerce Enthusiast

SHE SETS BOUNDARIES AND STICKS TO THEM

The Lady Hustler is a boundaries maven and she acknowledges the power establishing boundaries can have over her ability to stay energized, present and mother-freaking fierce.

So what are boundaries and what do they mean to the Lady Hustler?

Boundaries are different than creating a rule because a boundary is not a process or a tactic. No one is going to get reprimanded when breaking a boundary in the same way they may face consequences when breaking a rule. To the Lady Hustler, boundaries are setting levels of tolerance around what she chooses to let emotionally affect her.

Boundaries tend to be one of those gray areas for most people because they often come from an inner place of defining what is "acceptable for me." And what's acceptable to one Hustler, may be less acceptable to another Hustler. It is important to recognize both boundaries that exist (or don't yet exist) in the workplace and in your personal life. Sometimes these boundaries crossover in both environments, so the Lady Hustler takes note of how she is affected by each work/life balance quadrant.

For example, if the Lady Hustler is in a period of go, go, go and she is unable to implement some—if not all—of the daily R-E-S-P-E-C-T tactics because of unforeseen issues, she has the potential to go, go, go a little cray cray. With that, the Lady Hustler must abide by her boundaries to avoid exhaustion and burnout when she has a full week of meetings, outings and events. How's a sister going to kill it without some "me time" under her belt? That just 'aint happening…

A *rule* in this scenario may be that she can't be late to any planned work-related events. If so, she will face consequences from her boss. That said, she instead spends multiple days/nights in a row rushing from one event to the other thus making her a cranky little lady by the end of the week. She is unable to be present due to fatigue. Her mind is not on its "A" game. She's craving that moment of freedom.

She learns from this situation and realizes that long-term, overbooking herself is not logically sustainable, so she sets a *boundary* around becoming more mindful of her calendar to include breaks between the hustle.

Setting boundaries helps aid in her ability to feel empowered to make decisions best suited to her well-being. She evaluates her patterns and understands when shifts have to be made to live her most honest and fulfilling existence. This self-awareness drives her overall happiness—much more than crossing off items on that 'to-do' list.

DIY Tips

➤ Stop, drop and do a self-check-in roll. Think about what "rules" you have for yourself versus what "boundaries" you may be able to wrap around those rules. Why have you created that rule? How does measuring up to that rule make you feel? Is that rule serving you and/or is it realistic? {Phew, that's a lot to take in … meditate on that for a bit.}

➤ Think about how you may be setting yourself up for failure with one of your rules. A rule means there is a definitive "successful" or "not successful" outcome, so it could potentially cause a shame spiral if left unmet. Think about how having a better boundary (ie: gray area) instead of an unrealistic rule may be a better solution for you. So, for example, instead of saying, "I must go to bed at 10:30 p.m. every night, or else!" what may be better is to say to yourself, "I would like to aim to get eight hours of sleep per night because I know I am the most focused and a clear-headed human when I give my mind some rest." Then you will be more inclined to reward yourself for achieving that eight hours, instead of angering yourself if you don't hit the hay until 11:30 p.m.

➤ Think about your boundaries daily. The more you are able to allow room for improvement, the closer you will be able to hone in on your true needs.

➤ To recall previous boundaries or identify patterns, write it out! Keep notes in your phone or email yourself to have a frame of reference of the "last time something shitty happened." Sounds negative when framed this way, but we only feel frustrated and mad for a certain chunk of time and often let the same issues arise again without even evaluating their compound emotional effect. Keep an inventory of these situations to better identify your own patterns.

➤ Ultimately, establishing and understanding the power of boundaries leads to the day-to-day tendencies, rules and habits we accrue to respect our bodies and keep our minds intact. This helps to support our innermost desires, which can lead to heightened curiosity, newfound free time and the development of deeper connections.

LADY HUSTLER REAL TALK

"I so value the experiences I have had by being my own boss. I've only recently started this journey with Emily [my business partner] and have already learned so much about myself: how I manage budgets, how I manage time, how Emily and I are able to motivate each other and turn problems into solutions. It certainly makes me appreciate the work that my previous bosses had to tackle, because you quickly realize that the buck stops with you, and you're the one that needs to make the tough decisions. It's no easy process, but it is an incredible learning opportunity! I don't know if I'll ever stop learning from this experience—I sure hope not."

JESS PETERSON // Founder & Creative Director, Mighty Oak

"I maintain the hustle for a mixture of reasons. First ... God created me to be like the Energizer Bunny. I don't know where all of my energy comes from sometimes. I also have the tendency to be a people pleaser, so sometimes I also maintain the hustle because I don't want to let people down. I'm sure a lot of women can relate to that."

SARAH DEVRIES KURTENBACH // Consultant, Social Media & Startups

"There was a month where I was so anxious that I thought I was having a heart attack daily, my friends were mad at me for never being available to hang out, and I was constantly stressing over whether I was doing too much work or not enough. I got through it by allowing myself to not feel guilty when taking a break, but to see it as necessary to recharge my batteries."

LIZZY OKORO // Publisher & Editor-in-Chief, *BUNCH* Magazine

"Learn to say no. And say no when your gut tells you to. Sometimes the head lies. I know that for a fact."

MALENE ARVIN // Health Freak & Activewear Fashionista

"Often I feel compelled to answer work emails while sitting in class, or text a co-worker while on break ... but I've been trying to maintain my focus on what's in front of me, and keep my responsibilities from bleeding over into one another. Wherever I am, I try to be focused on the task at hand and devote all of my energy to the person I'm working with or the project in which I'm involved."

JANE CORBETT // Graduate Student, Clinical Psychology

"I do have a problem over-committing and need to designate more 'me time' during the week. I make my weekends super-exclusive and low-key and try my best to

get all of my social obligations out of the way during the week. Then I can be super-thoughtful of who I spend my time with on the weekends."

EMILY MERRELL // Events Manager, INTERMIX & City Society NYC Women's Networking

"I used to say yes to everything—every opportunity, shift at work, date with a friend, extra project, etc. But that didn't work for me very well. I'd end up feeling resentful or tired or burned out. Now instead of 'doing it all,' I prioritize enjoying my life every single day. I really try hard not to take on too many tasks or extra responsibilities. I only say yes to the things I really want to do. And then I can do them really, really well."

KARA LEVINE // Pilates Instructor & Holistic Health Coach

CHAPTER 4: YOU CAN THRIVE LIKE HER TOO … AIN'T NOBODY GON' STOP YOU NOW, BOO

Now you know exactly how she makes it work.

1. She's a planoholic,

2. She respects herself,

3. She is curious and strives to better herself,

4. She has a shit-ton of fun with great people, and

5. She manifests for the future by allowing herself to remain as curious and as open-minded as possible.

We all have at least one of these qualities and, often, we have more than one. So what stops us from igniting the fire to get real with ourselves by being true to our authentic beliefs and desires?

It's simple … ourselves.

Gah! It can be a pain in the tukhus to come to grips with this, but there really is no difference between the Lady Hustler and {ahem} you. Sure, she may incorporate daily hacks or tricks of the trade that may be different from our own, but she looks at her life with the glass half full, is aware she is in control of "what she can control" and keeps on keeping on every day. All of this comes down to having a positive mindset. This holistic routine helps her maintain her grind and, in turn, grants her the ability to thrive each day. She may just be farther along in her journey than you are, which is OK, because we are exactly where we need to be today. {And don't you forget it!}

We've moved to new cities, met new people, experienced the ups and downs of romantic relationships when we've least expected it, and changed the direction of our careers. Each event happened for a reason, at a specific time in our lives, on a particular day and in an order in which we never expected.

"Well, she must be missing something, right? She doesn't sleep, right? Or, wait, how is she always so happy?"

You know what? She doesn't have it all and she certainly doesn't have life "figured out," but she has aligned herself with situations that feel right to her and she's the ultimate gut listener.

Identifying your ability to embrace unanticipated moments is just as important as packing your calendar with meetings galore. Our goals should be, and can be, achieved in the same 40 hours as the "typical" full-time work week. The Lady Hustler doesn't possess anything that you, my dear, don't also have inside of you. The difference is she's an individual who's been able to tap into her innermost passion and listen to her inner calling which makes her jump for joy. Through the non-negotiable tips and tricks she incorporates into her day, she's able to have better clarity to take the control of her life and thrive.

YOU CAN THRIVE EVERY DAY TOO

The principles we discussed in this book are easily broken down into learning how to T-H-R-I-V-E every day.

T = Thoughtfulness

Care for yourself and be thoughtful toward others. Pay yourself and someone else a compliment at least once time each day. Karma will come back in spades.

H = Hustle yourself happy

Hustle and be an action-taker. You have the tools, it's just a matter of figuring out what works for you to check tasks off your list and, in turn, you will discover your own way to finance your growth wisely. You will be following a path you love and also have the time and freedom to incorporate activities worth smiling about.

R = Residual growth

Realize that growth is residual and will not happen overnight. Rome wasn't built in a day. Integrating elements of inspiration, diversifying your income, remaining curious and having a clear vision will enable you to have a balanced and more sustainable life—both fiscally and emotionally. Commit to learning and allow this growth to emerge. Put yourself in situations that ignite your dreams and add to your personal development.

I = Inspire

Speaking of inspiration: as much as you have been inspired by other's successes, you have your own story to share. It's easy to spend hours ingesting inspirational messages from others to open your mind and, while this is necessary to evolve, know you have the power to inspire others along their journey as well. Your story is important and you are doing a disservice to others by not sharing your experiences.

V = Know your Value

You are worth it! When you genuinely believe and respect yourself, others will do the same. Your view of yourself should not be clouded by fear, worry, or doubt. You have the power within you to reach your highest potential. You are important. You are enough.

E = Empowerment

Constantly feel empowered. Think about your decisions and if your gut is telling you something, listen to it. Your gut tells you what is right for you.

Lastly, smile all the freaking time, surround yourself with happy people and you will not only become a Lady Hustler, you will continually learn more about yourself and your own thriving recipe in the process.

LET AUTHENTICITY BE YOUR GUIDE

After learning about the daily tips and tricks and, of course, what internal fire makes the Lady Hustler "Thrive in Her Hustle," the last piece that sets her apart is her insatiable ability to create an aura of irresistibility. Her purpose is so deeply grounded she only commits to activities that contribute to her overall wellbeing and growth. Her true, authentic self shines so darn bright, it leaves others attracted to her energy. We all know now, this is because *She Makes it Work*. She's created a lifestyle and profession that works solely for her. And you can, too!

Discovering your path is not easy. We are in a unique era in time where "moving to the big city" is no longer a necessity to fulfill you.

With the ability to grow a lifestyle anywhere—we are fortunate to be in a position where we can have our "lifestyle cake" and eat it too. However, this becomes somewhat confusing to the average millennial as we're entering the real world, attempting to find that "it job." We are constantly reminded through social media of our peers' flashy careers and travels, so much so that it is easy to feel like we are missing something. This reminds us how important it is to find joy in our daily lives, but it also is confusing because it pushes us to ask the age-old questions...

What is my purpose?

What is my worth?

What do I want my legacy to be?

Quite often, the answer is right in front of us. But, we are overwhelmed with messages of self-doubt and are influenced by the doubts and fears of others to a point where it can make us feel small beyond belief. But we have to be committed to owning our hobbies, passions and/or a job that feels uniquely our own. Considering a huge chunk of our waking hours are spent working our buns off, it's essential to make a commitment to ourselves and to choose to find our own version of happy. At work, this means something that keeps you engaged, allows for you to lead, and is at least 90% toxic-free. Strive for this fulfillment.

If you still feel unhappy in a career and need to do a pulse check, explore how you are R-E-S-P-E-C-T-ing yourself outside of the work environment. Then, see how your self-awareness and confidence could be influencing the "person" you allow to show up to your work environment—or anywhere else for that matter.

Allow your authentic self to be present. The Lady Hustler has that "wow factor," not because she's Beyoncé or the CEO of a company, but because she enters the world with her heart open. Her soul's mission is worn right on her sleeve, regardless of power and regardless of whether she's an introvert or extrovert. In fact, many of our Lady Hustlers have deemed themselves introverts despite having seemingly outward careers.

Be genuine in your approach and authentic to yourself.

Though these words are synonymous, challenge yourself to see the difference between them.

Be externally genuine and internally authentic.

Check in with yourself often to ensure you are continuing to tell yourself a true story about YOU and are eliminating the distractions. Then, be genuine in your messaging, your love, your support and your honesty toward others.

Lastly, don't be ashamed of your interests. Own them. They are part of what makes you 'you.' Have a "coming out" party and prove that you are the biggest believer in you there ever was. Your tribe will support you.

At the end of the day, most Lady Hustlers are in search of finding true freedom and empowerment. They do this through the T-H-R-I-V-E concept, by balancing productivity with wellness tools, and by generating strong human connection. True freedom will only be achieved by discovering your own true authentic calling. Go through the process of finding this calling.

Choose to be you. Choose to be authentic. Then you can be your own version of the Lady Hustler.

WORDS TO INSPIRE FROM THE AUTHOR

Today is a new day. Wear new clothes, paint your nails, and part your hair in the middle for a change. Let yesterday's look fall to the wayside. Hold on to the lessons and memories from days and years past, but enter today with a fresh face.

Turn your passions into reality. It can be done. Discovering your "why" is the first step.

Know that people will disagree with your calling and there will be many naysayers along the way. They are afraid for you and will try to bring you down with their own fears. Smile and keep moving forward toward the direction of your dreams.

Lose control every now and then.

Procrastination is fear manifesting as excuses which delay your progress.

Spend time with people who make you feel expansive. Much like we wouldn't fill up our tummies with icky foods, we also don't want to fill our minds with toxic opinions. A vibrant meal will help you glow much like a loved one or friend with a happy demeanor will enable you to make happy decisions for your mental health.

Don't shine your light into a dark hole. The darkness will absorb and draw each and every glimmer from your being.

Be in hot pursuit of your dreams. Be honest with yourself. Take action, and keep your eye on the prize.

You are not a blank canvas ... you have stories and a chemical makeup that is uniquely you. You just need to really listen and learn how to pull those elements out of your being to share with others. You are doing yourself a disservice by not sharing your strengths.

Lastly, you are a Hustler. Make shit happen every day. You have the power to create and shape the life you want to live. Write your dreams down and make them come to life. Your future thriving self will thank you.

RESOURCES

GOAL SETTING

➤ **Your "Why"** – Goals are important, but getting grounded in your purpose as to why you are hustling will continue to help support your goals. Each and every action should be challenged with a, "Why am I doing this? How does this make me feel?" When you identify your "why," you can take on the world!

➤ **SMART Goals** stand for creating goals that are (1) Specific, (2) Measurable, (3) Attainable, (4) Realistic and (5) Timely. When creating a new goal, consider each of these items to ensure there's no stopping you from achieving away.

➤ **Big Rocks** – Setting "Big Rocks" goals allows you to think about what you want to achieve in life overall, so the smaller goals will become elements of the bigger picture. Basically, hard charging for your big goals will help you avoid excuses by filling in the gaps with the smaller, less game-changing goals.

➤ **Dream Board** – These are your visual goals. A dream board is the space for you to create something beautiful to display within view. Oftentimes when you believe something is beautiful and visualize this positively for a future life, your dreams will come to fruition when least expected.

PRODUCTIVITY

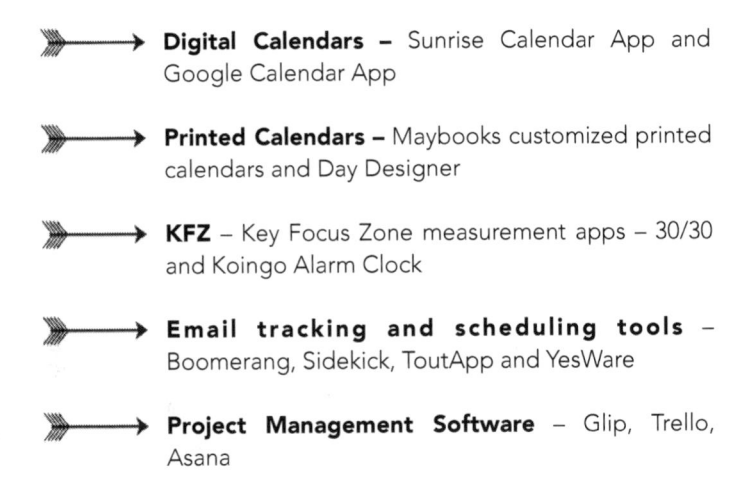

- **Digital Calendars –** Sunrise Calendar App and Google Calendar App

- **Printed Calendars –** Maybooks customized printed calendars and Day Designer

- **KFZ** – Key Focus Zone measurement apps – 30/30 and Koingo Alarm Clock

- **Email tracking and scheduling tools** – Boomerang, Sidekick, ToutApp and YesWare

- **Project Management Software** – Glip, Trello, Asana

QUICK NEWS SOURCES

Need 2 Know, Daily Beast, The Skimm, Ann Friedman Weekly, Flipboard
*** Can sign up for all when doing a search on Google

HEALTHY LIVING

- **Glycemic Index** – Index of the effect of food on blood sugar levels. The higher the index of sugar-containing foods, the higher the crash and spike. For more information, visit: www.glycemicindex.com.

➤ **Community Shared Agriculture shares** (CSAs) – For more information on locally sourced agriculture, visit: www.localharvest.org/csa.

➤ **Dirty Dozen** – Always purchase these fruits and vegetables local and organic as they are often the most affected by harmful chemicals and pesticides: apples, strawberries, grapes, celery, peaches, spinach, peppers, nectarines, cucumber, tomatoes, snap peas, potatoes, blueberries.

➤ **Clean Fifteen** – If you are a bit strapped for cash and find that the Clean Fifteen is more affordable, then these items are less harmful when they aren't organic: avocados, sweet corn, pineapples, cabbage, sweet peas (frozen), onions, asparagus, mangoes, papayas, kiwi, eggplant, grapefruit, cantaloupe (domestic), cauliflower, sweet potatoes.

➤ **Suggested Vitamins – USANA Health Sciences** are high-quality, pharmaceutical-grade vitamins, minerals and antioxidants formulated to improve health at the cellular level. I so believe in these products that I decided to choose USANA as my preferred product partner! To learn more, about your individual vitamin needs, visit: katiecorc.usana.com.

➤ **Exercise** – DoYogaWithMe.com, Grooker.com and Greatist has a fabulous list by visiting: greatist.com/move/best-free-workout-videos-youtube.

➤ **Meditation** – HeadSpace meditation app, or free guided meditations on SoundCloud.

PRINCIPLES

T-H-R-I-V-E Every Day concept – Coined by Katie Corcoran, this concept teaches that in order to have the best of days you must incorporate (1) Thoughtfulness, (2) Hustle, (3) Residual Growth, (4) Inspire others, (5) Know your Value, and (6) Feel Empowered in your gut. For more information about this concept and to take the #THRIVErrday challenge, visit www.katiecorc.com

Law of Detachment – According to the Chopra Center, this principle revolves around removing yourself from any outcome. This means you are taking action and caring for others because you desire to and not for a reward. For more information, visit: www.chopra.com/the-law-of-detachment.

Ubuntu – A South African philosophy that translates to "the belief in a universal bond of sharing that connects all humanity." For more information, visit: www.drfranklipman.com/q-and-as-on-ubuntu.

EDUCATION

Institute for Integrative Nutrition – The world's largest nutrition school, empowering you to launch an exciting new career and build a life you love through healthy holistic living. Core concepts include evaluating an individual's "Primary Foods" including happiness and balance within (1) career, (2) exercise, (3) relationships, and (4) spirituality. When all are in balance, then typically we make better "Secondary Food" decisions which is the food we actually put into our mouths. then, IIN also coined the concept of "Bioindividuality" where on person's nourishment may be another person's poison. Certified coaches work with clients through primary foods and discuss bioindividuality and lifestyle adjustments. For more information visit bit.ly/Join_IIN_KatieCorc.

New Self-Health Movement – Learn from some of my peer authors about all books wellness-related through our community page by visiting here: thenewself-healthmovement.com/homepage.

#IThriveToday Challenge – Connect through this group lead by myself and Guramrit Khalsa about the power of thriving by bursting through fears, talking all things goal setting, finances and passion-identifying galore by gaining access here: http://bit.ly/IThriveToday.

SUGGESTED READING LIST – Take a look-see here: bit.ly/KatieSuggestedReads.

MEET THE LADY HUSTLERS

JESSY DOVER is a Designer, Creative Director & Co-Founder of functional handbag company Dagne Dover. She studied fashion design at Parsons School of Design and after a series of jobs and internships at Armani Exchange, Coach and Nili Lotan, she found her passion in designing handbags. Since 2012, she has built and created Dagne Dover with co-founders Deepa Gandhi and Melissa Shin. For more information, visit: www.dagnedover.com (Pages 42, 72, 108)

LIZZY OKORO is the publisher and editor-in-chief of *BUNCH* Magazine, an independent magazine that serves as a "Guide for the Daring Creative." Inspired by the rising creative class that she interacted with while living in New York, Lizzy reworked her plans to pursue a career in international affairs to focus on a career in publishing. Lizzy can now be found in her hometown of LA, reading through piles of other magazines, Snapchatting videos of her puppy, Instagramming food pictures, and thinking of her next big hustle. For more information, visit: www.bunchmag.com (Pages 41, 80, 97, 126)

SARAH DEVRIES KURTENBACH is a social media and tech startup expert who has worked for a top Facebook preferred marketing developer for over five years. Starting as the second employee, she helped grow the company to a multi-million dollar business, brought the company through an acquisition and has worked post-acquisition within a large Fortune 500 media company. She has strategized, built content, put together process plans, run digital media, analyzed data and brought success to hundreds of advertisers in addition to being on the board of multiple non-profits and other organizations to lead their digital and social efforts. She has spoken at several digital media conferences around the country. Sarah recently moved from NYC to South Dakota to marry the love of her life, and has a passion for helping business owners succeed in the ever-changing digital and social space. For more information, visit: www.theKBgroup.com (Pages 36, 57, 67, 79, 102, 114, 125)

KATHY BACON is the founder of Dress for Success in Denver, CO. She is enthusiastic about creating kindness throughout the universe. Kathy hosts a radio show called Pay it Forward Radio and also hosted Fashion Forward radio for two years. Kathy is rebranding to include reading for authors, voiceover work and finding a new home for Pay it Forward Radio that will syndicate her show. When Kathy is not out in the community creating kindness she is with her husband and two cats, Pearl and Enzo. She has three grown children and one grandson named Logan. Kathy loves being out in nature and riding her bike. For more information, visit: www.kathybacon.com (Pages 58, 103)

MALENE ARVIN is the owner of YO STUDIOS and YO WEAR and lives in Denmark. She is a personal trainer, yoga teacher, health coach, runner, passionate dancer, and new mother. For more information, visit: www.yostudios.dk / www.yowear.dk (Pages 49, 66, 79, 90, 120, 126)

GURAMRIT KHALSA lives, breathes and sleeps health and wellness. Her love for wellness fuels her passion for cooking, yoga, meditation and spirituality. Guramrit is a holistic health counselor, certified by the Institute for Integrative Nutrition and a graduate of the S.I. Newhouse School of Public Communications at Syracuse University, where she earned a B.S.

in magazine journalism. As a holistic health counselor, she places a strong emphasis on self-love and self-care and ways to infuse love and gratitude into all aspects of daily life. Guramrit just published her first of many books, *Yogi Eats: A Delicious Journey to Nourishing Your Soul*, as a manual for inspiring others to infuse yogic principles into their lives while also utilizing their kitchens as a hub for wellness (Pages 50, 57)

MICHELA ARAMINI is the founder of The Lovely It Girl, a personal-brand consulting boutique in New York dedicated to inspiring and empowering you to become the bold, beautiful, brilliant It Girl you were born to be. As a personal brand consultant and "it girl" mentor, Michela works with entrepreneurial women helping them create bespoke personal brands that clarify and communicate their "It," connect them to their clique, and ultimately empower them to make a living doing what they love. For more information, visit: thelovelyitgirl.com (Pages 23, 35, 49, 66)

TALLY MACK is a fifth-generation pawnbroker living in a software world. She and her father run Bravo Store Systems, a pawn platform that elevates small and medium-size businesses to the next level. For more information, visit: www.Buya.com (Pages 28, 72, 76, 79, 120)

CLARA LOFARO is a Toronto-raised singer songwriter who resides in Brooklyn, New York. She realized her abilities for harmonies at an early age when she began singing in a local community church. She then continued to study and perform music throughout her formative and high school years before accepting a scholarship at the Berklee College of Music in Boston. Her current EP release, "Air Lift Me," follows three earlier LPs: Perfekt World, Black & Blue Pearl and Self-Titled LP, all of which were written by Lofaro. "Air Lift Me" contains the hit single "Born To Love You," charting at #21 on the Billboard Club Charts. Her songs have aired on various TV networks including NBC, ABC, MTV and Lifetime. She has performed alongside Stevie Nicks, Edwin McCain, Kimberly Locke and Jeffrey Gaines, and was the featured vocalist in the Disney Super Bowl commercial "When You Wish Upon a Star" featuring MVP players of the NFL team. She was also in a national Vanity Fair Napkins "Wipe on a Smile" campaign featuring her single "Just Smile." For more information, visit www.claralofaro.com (Pages 24, 35, 50, 58, 80, 84, 108)

ANDREA HOOD is a certified holistic health coach, business mentor, and co-founder of Wildly Vibrant Living. Andrea is a passionate foodie and localvore who loves playing in the kitchen and whipping up delicious, healthy meals. Andrea's purpose in life is to empower women to feel comfortable in their own skin and take charge of their financial independence. For more information about how you can live a more empowered life, visit: www.andreahood.com (Pages 50, 58)

EMILY MERRELL was born in Florida and moved to Connecticut at the ripe age of 12. As a middle schooler she harnessed her skill of doubling as Frida Kahlo, and after being asked what Latin American country she yielded from she decided to study Spanish and communications (girl needed to communicate!) at a small liberal arts university in Ohio. Upon graduating from Denison University she moved to Buenos Aires to master her Spanish and worked in various industries (ask her about Malbec). Following her return to New York City she landed in the fashion world working at Ralph Lauren, Club Monaco, Tory Burch, and is currently at Intermix. In her free time you can find her exploring new restaurants, drinking bold bottles of wine, taking early morning workout classes, planning her next trip or planning her next networking event through her NYC-based women's networking community called City Society. (Pages 41, 84, 104, 107, 127)

MELANIE COHN works as a social media manager for a large QSR brand, leading strategy, content, influencer activation and paid advertising. Previously, she worked at a Boston advertising agency supervising consumer engagement strategies for national CPG, tourism and restaurant brands. Melanie is also the founder of Young Women in Digital, a Boston-based networking group of over 1,000 young marketing professionals. YWD hosts creative and pressure-free events and classes for professionals to mix and mingle, gain digital skills and hear from top speakers in the digital marketing world. Melanie was awarded as a BostInno 50 on Fire nominee in 2013 in the marketing and advertising category among top marketers in Boston. For more information, visit: www.youngwomenindigital.com (Pages 42, 97, 115)

JESS PETERSON is the founder and creative director of Mighty Oak, a boutique studio specializing in stop-motion animation, hand-drawn illustration, concise messaging and workshops for female founders. For the past 10 years she's worked in music and the visual arts, helping artists, musicians and cultural institutions find their voice. Past work collaborations have included the Children's Museum of the Arts, Dumbo Arts Festival, The Flaming Lips, Brooklyn Arts Council, and *The New York Times*. When she's not creating stories, communications plans or workshops, you can find her hosting an event for HATCH, a monthly meet-up for creative female founders. Or find her behind a wedding DJ booth, spinning records with her husband. For more information, visit: www.mightyoakgrows.com (Pages 35, 113, 125)

AMY LEVIN is the founder and creative director of the distinguished CollegeFashionista, an online publication showcasing the latest fashion styles and trends on college campuses around the world. It was while studying abroad in London that Amy discovered the true influence of street style on the fashion industry. Back at Indiana University for her senior year, Amy noticed a gap in college-oriented blogs, and thus CollegeFashionista was born. The site quickly spread to other campuses, turning her newly found hobby into a full-blown career. Since its initial launch in 2009, CollegeFashionista has now grown to encompass 500-plus campuses worldwide and is home to thousands of contributors. For more information, visit: www.collegefashionista.com (Pages 28, 67, 103)

HALEY HUGHES BRYAN is originally from Atlanta, Georgia, where she graduated from the Georgia Institute of Technology with a degree in management in 2008. After graduation she moved to New York to work in account management for advertising agencies Ogilvy & Mather and mcgarrybowen, and later for an ad tech company, RadiumOne. She moved to San Francisco two years ago with her husband and started her own e-commerce women's sleepwear company, Terrimae. For more information, visit: www.terrimae.com (Pages 24, 43, 96)

STEPHANIE MAY WILSON is equal parts writer and celebrator who believes that even Tuesday is worthy of a champagne toast. She believes in the healing power of a warm cup of coffee and a place to let your guard down. For her, that space is her online blog where she shares stories of big adventures and small moments with friends and strangers alike. Follow her on Instagram and Twitter (@smaywilson), and check out her first book, *The Lipstick Gospel*. For more information, visit: StephanieMayWilson.com (Pages 34, 98, 103, 114, 119)

KARA LEVINE is a New York City-based pilates instructor, holistic health coach, and founder of Blush Wellness—a company that provides personalized programming for brides looking to lose weight, get in shape and get healthy for their big day. Kara's favorite thing is helping others get fit and happy. Some of her other favorite things include rainbow sprinkles, running in Hudson River Park, and singing with her a capella group. For other healthy tips, recipes and more information about Blush, visit www.blushwellness.org (Pages 23, 107, 115, 119, 127)

BRANDI SHIGLEY is on a mission to turn dreamers into doers. Starting her first company 15 years ago with her handbag business, B.Shigley Designs, Shigley has learned the ups and downs of being an independent designer and now focuses much of her time on Fashion Denver, a business she started 10 years ago to help designers build their businesses. Through the production of fashion markets, fashion shows and business development, Shigley is helping to put Denver on the map for fashion. It's not just fashion that she's passionate about, but artists, musicians and creative people with a desire to take their passion to the next level. She has been featured on CNN Money, International Design Magazine, and has also been a featured speaker with TEDx. For more information, visit: www.dowhatyoulove.us (Page 50)

TAYLOR ROCKOFF recently received her master's in international development focusing on education and conflict from American University's School of International Service. She is currently working as a Fellow at the International Peace & Security Institute in Washington, DC, where she is planning for their experiential training The Hague in international justice and post-conflict transitions. Promoting a holistic approach to health and wellness is another passion of Taylor's. She has worked in various capacities since 2010 in the health and wellness industry, mostly as a yoga instructor but also as a boot camp coach, and most recently as a fitness business consultant for Rock Solid Health. She received her first yoga certification in 2010 with Corepower Yoga, and her 200-hour certification from Yogaview in Chicago. Taylor also holds a certification as a fitness nutrition specialist. (Pages 72, 96, 102, 120)

JANE CORBETT* is a graduate student pursuing her doctorate in clinical psychology in the NYC area. Throughout her training she has worked in a psychiatric hospital, college counseling center, a substance abuse treatment facility, and in a NYC homeless shelter for young adults. (Pages 76, 90, 126)

*Name has been changed for privacy

SPECIAL THANKS

MY LADY HUSTLERS – You deserve your own round of applause. You were patient with me as I took you on this twisty, turny ride that included featuring and learning from your behaviors. Through many emails and inspiring conversations it gives me great pleasure to share your stories and professional overlaps! Thank you for being rockin' individuals and staying empowered in your hustle. I feel your triumphs just as much as I can relate to your struggle. Your passion is contagious and I get a charge from your spark. Just know, you have the biggest cheerleader in me, and I know you have contributed to inspiring each and every reader in *She Makes It Work*.

DAD - With no one really to hold me accountable for the completion of this book I have you, and will always have you, to continue to encourage and push me on the sidelines to remind me "to just get it done." With my overly analytical mind that doubts every single word and meets tremendous resistance, I have you to thank for being my teacher—making sure deadlines are met despite reaching [many] moments of doubt. Thank you for teaching me to never arrive, but to continue to strive for better in my life's journey.

MOM - You are my dream cheerleader. You remind me that no one is perfect, we all have feelings and also show me that, as humans, we continue to learn at all ages. I have gone through some of the same self-discoveries as you at the same times, and I am so honored to share that bond with you. Then, thank you for being a diligent editor. For challenging the phonetics, staying up late nights thinking about structure, and integrating some of the learnings from my book into your own entrepreneurial dreams months before others were able to get their paws on a copy. I have you to thank for always lighting up when I share new ideas with you and for also reminding me the sky is the limit.

MY SISTERS & BRO – Hannah, Gill, Lindsey, Aimee and Ryan— for still loving and laughing with me after letting my older-sister, hustlin' ass boss you around for years. Thank you for challenging me and reminding me that, though I'm older, life is not always my way or the highway. I am fond of your uniqueness and hope you all know you are VERY different and please honor and appreciate your own talents and special personalities. Please always know your big sis is on your team, and I may show it in strange ways like snuggling on the couch, or texting you a weird picture, or even by {ahem} pushing you to strive higher. This is the case because I believe in you and want you to look at every experience as an opportunity to grow into your own special you.

GRAM R - The original "Lady Hustler." Thank you for showing me what it means to be a strong, empowering, "do it yourself"-type. Your unconditional love, respect, and support have kept me thinking positively all of these years. Thank you for always making me feel special.

RENEE & TONY - My second parents! Thank you for being a huge part of my childhood, life, and "modern family" unit. You are the best!

FAMILY — Kathy, Joan, Steve, Randy, Brian, Grandma Joan, Mary, Roman, Popo, Ba, Nini, Karen, Diane & Mike- Love to you all!

JESSY – My oh my, what can happen in just a year is remarkable. I am so lucky to have you as an NYC bestie. Thank you for taking the time to literally talk me through each and every scenario included in this book. Thank you for constantly reminding me when I'm in a phase of tremendous stress, it's probably best to get some sleep, go to SoulCycle, shut down my computer and have some fun. It's been a lifesaver to create new memories and grow alongside you at this time in our "quarter-life crisis" moments. I credit a large portion of that evolution to this phase in our friendship. Cheers to more books, new ideas, handbags, more travels and new companies.

TALLY – You are a star. You have been the MK to my A since the first day of college. You are the most loyal, positive and encouraging friend a girl could ask for. You are my family. I can't thank you enough for dropping all of your plans when I'm in need of a Tally vent-session at any moment. You are one-of-a-kind and hold such a special place in my heart.

TAYLOR – Thank you for reminding me to find the imperfect in the perfect and if you're not infectiously laughing through life, then you ain't living! I love your ability to look at life freely and to constantly live in a state of fulfilling the passions that you love. I will never worry about "Tay doing Tay" because you are so grounded in your purpose.

STEVIE - You are the funniest and most loyal friend and I can always count on you to give it to me "straight up for Lady Kale." Thank you for encouraging me to bring out the sass and for reminding me to laugh all the time.

GURAMRIT – My accountability buddy and fellow #IThriveToday coach. Your passion is contagious and you always know when to reach out with a positive quote and/or send love my way in moments of need [without knowing it was a moment of need].

ANDREA, LIZ, SARAH & JESSICA – You four crack me up. To my sassy, foxy, vibrant and hilarious health coach besties. Thank you!

LAYSA - You are a gem. Thank you for pushing me to finish this book, by holding me accountable for jumping full force into my passion and for keeping me sane during tremendous transition.

I am so lucky to have met you through IIN and so honored to call you an accountability partner.

CLARA – Whether you know it or not, you have been such a mentor to me by demonstrating your commitment to being an independent creative. You are a true testament that our hearts and guts do not lie. I greatly look up to your strength.

LEAH – Roomie! Thank you so much for giving me the space to work freely and accepting my strange writing habits when they strike at odd hours. You are amazing.

MAN FRIEND SUPPORTERS – For the number of times I heard, "Even though I'm a guy, I can't wait to learn from your book. Oh, and can I get a signed copy?" You guys crack me up and, yes, signed copy coming your way. Thank you for your willingness to learn and support this gal doing her thang.

ADVERTISING START-UP JOB – Shout out to the full-time work that allowed for me to be a side-hustler. Thank you for teaching me what it's like to build a company from the ground up, create positions, build teams, remain flexible during management adjustments, and also showing me how to communicate work both internally and externally.

INSTITUTE FOR INTEGRATIVE NUTRITION – Wow. Thank you from the bottom of my heart for the love and community this program has cultivated. I have like-minded friends from around the world because of this school, and I feel like the luckiest lady to continue to learn from leaders and teachers about well-being and personal growth. To the Ambassador team, Lindsey Smith & IIN Founder Joshua Rosenthal for pushing me to make this book happen. I am forever grateful.

USANA HEALTH SCIENCES // THRIVE TRIBE & ENLIGHTENED LIVING FAMILY – You have all individually helped me better understand that business is still important when building our coaching careers. You remind me it's important to remain grounded when making financial decisions for growth to allow for freedom to support a lifestyle to continue to do this unconventional, freedom-inspired work. Elizabeth Rider, you are a gem, and thank you for leading our team and seeing the potential in me to stay committed, for challenging me to get over my fears and resistance, and showing me the power is inside of each individual to choose a life you want for you. This is a perfect daily mantra I remind myself to follow through your guidance.

TO MY LADY HUSTLERS IN TRAINING – To quote *Strengths Finder 2.0* by Tom Rath: "You cannot be anything you want to be, but you can be a lot more of who you already are." Keep on honing in on your purpose and you too will be just as powerful as those you admire. But know that the T-H-R-I-V-E concept will empower you to keep on keeping on and to believe in you. I do and will support you along the way.

SPOTIFY – More specifically, Jon Bellion for the first half of the book and to "Music Friday" and "Discover" during the second, third, fourth, etc. pieces of this book. These songs are the perfect mixture to get in the ZONE before, during, and after every section was meticulously butchered, rewritten, and during the agonizing moments spent formatting, doubting myself, and second {or triple} guessing each and every sentence.

SOULCYCLE & CLASSPASS – For keeping me accountable to stay on top of my sweat game and to the inpsiring fitness leaders to help take my mind far away from the stresses of the day. At each class there's an opportunity to quit, to lighten the dial on my spin bike, to start to let the "I can't do it" mind creep into my practice, but conquering the mini accomplishments to make it through the hard moments nine times out of 10 have influenced the growth of this book. It's funny that when you try hard to get your mind to STOP thinking about something, the more inclined you are to fill that space with new killer ideas.

FREE, FUNCTIONING WIFI – 'Cause, yeah. Work from anywhere.

SELF-HELP BOOKS – This probably doesn't surprise you, right? I've read many and have had "ah has" from all reads. For a list of book recommendations, check out the resource section and/or head on over to my Amazon store to see if any are a fit for you to pick up and read.

COFFEE OF ALL VARIETIES – Iced almond milk lattes, cold brew, dirty chais, Vietnamese iced coffees, matcha lattes and more.

TRAVELS – This manuscript has been in coffee shops, hotels, planes, trains and automobiles all over the United States, but the greatest breakthroughs can be credited to time spent in San Francisco, Ho Chi Minh City, Vietnam and Montauk, NY. It's amazing where the mind can go when it's out of a routine and free.

HOW I MAKE IT WORK Notes

(To remember all the good shit you just learned.)

HOW I MAKE IT WORK Notes

HOW I MAKE IT WORK Notes

CONTACT

WWW.KATIECORC.COM

INSTAGRAM / TWITTER
@KATIECORC
@THRIVE_TRIBE

ABOUT THE AUTHOR

Katie Corcoran is a vibrant Lady Hustler who is passionate about helping others thrive in their careers and personal lives. As a healthy-living expert and lifestyle coach, Katie helps others master happiness to experience residual growth on a daily basis. She does this through her one-on-one business mentoring program and group trainings to teach women how they too can unlock their inner hustling recipe.

Katie's unique approach to living an authentic and thriving life is credited to her education at the Institute for Integrative Nutrition. She graduated in 2012 as a certified health and lifestyle coach. To add to her expertise and Lady Hustler status, Katie has a five-year background in brand strategy, digital marketing and advertising, mixed with DIY PR work for indie artists.

She currently lives in Brooklyn, NY, and can be found sipping on a latte while jamming to the latest hip-hop song, her eyes wide open to the intricacies of a local neighborhood's charm. When she's not working on her hustle or exploring new 'hoods, she enjoys escaping to the raw spirit that can only be found in nature, where she resets and rewinds.

Made in the USA
Middletown, DE
08 February 2016